The Story of
PARKEND
a Forest of Dean Village

Ralph Anstis

This remarkable picture, taken by the Coleford photographer F. E. Jones, provides the first known view of the Parkend Royal Branch, as it wound its way up through this industrialised part of the village to reach Castlemain and Parkend Royal collieries. In the foreground, the whitewashed building is the offices of the Parkend Deep Navigation Coal Company and was built as workshops, stables and yard for the Parkend Coal Company. The large building to its left is the British Lion Inn, now demolished. The two blocks of houses on the right are on the area known as 'Mount Pleasant' and in the centre distance can be seen the houses along Fancy Row, on the far side of the cricket green. York Lodge can just be made out in the right background and the timber yard behind the trees in the far left distance. The photograph dates from around 1905.

courtesy Peggy Preest

Above: Looking across New Road from the cricket green circa 1930, with Castlemain pumping engine on the right and Parkend Royal Colliery just visible in the centre background. The route of the Parkend Royal Branch can be clearly seen above the roofs of the houses. The large detached house on the left has always been known by locals as 'the 1910 house', although it was actually named 'Forest Vale', which can just be discerned in the glass above the front door.

Front cover: Parkend station in about 1905, from the top of the iron-works cinder tips.

First published in Great Britain in 1982 by
The Forest Bookshop, Coleford, Gloucestershire
First published in this edition in 1998 by Lightmoor Press
Revised and reprinted with extra photographic content, 2009

© Ralph Anstis & Lightmoor Press

British Library Cataloguing-in-Publication data.
A catalogue record for this book is available from the British Library.

ISBN 9781899889044

Published by Lightmoor Press
Unit 144b Lydney Industrial Estate, Harbour Road, Lydney, Gloucestershire GL15 4EJ

Printed in England by Information Press, Eynsham, Oxfordshire
www.informationpress.com

Contents

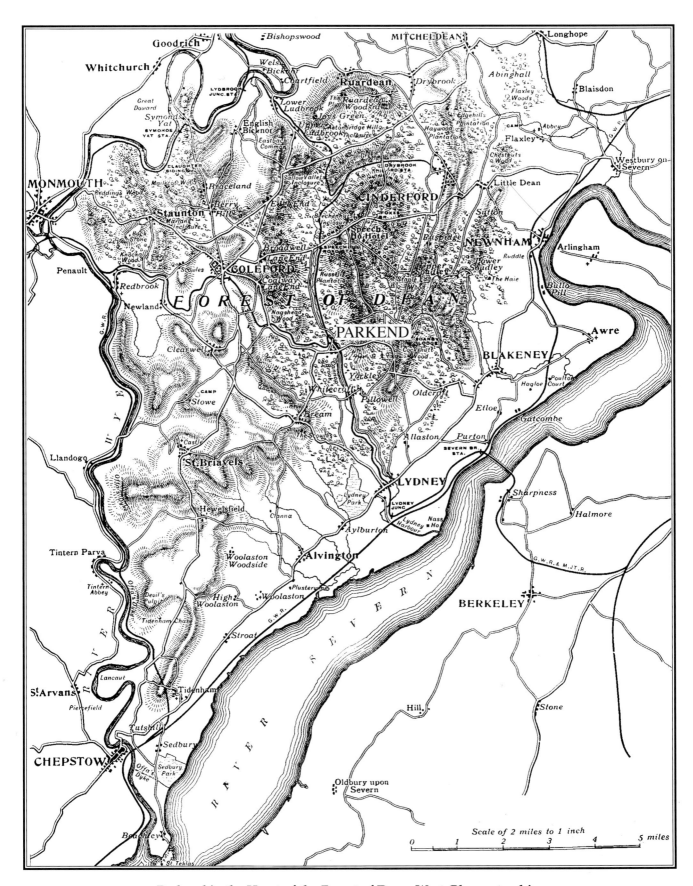

Parkend in the Heart of the Forest of Dean, West Gloucestershire.

Foreword
by
Dr. Cyril Hart O.B.E.
HM Senior Verderer of the Royal Forest of Dean

Most of the books and booklets relating to the Royal Forest of Dean are either specialist in nature or wide-sweeping - being generally a condensed history which, though factual, interesting and useful, of necessity pays little attention to detail. Such a treatment of history obviously comprises only a microcosm of the history of our Forest's many towns and villages – the time-consuming research and the restricted printed space having denied adequate individual treatment. Hence it is only by long, detailed research that an individual town, village or other location can be adequately treated, enabling the story to be told of its origin, development and inhabitants - and how and under what conditions they have worked, lived and worshipped.

Ralph Anstis has accomplished for Parkend (a truly and typical Forest village) what should or could be done likewise for other villages. First drawing upon the published general information on our Forest, he has then set for himself the task of researching the individual history of the village which he has made his second home, Parkend. The fulfilment of his task has resulted in a fascinating and detailed history which will give pleasure and satisfaction not only to residents and neighbours of Parkend but also to readers from a wider field.

I commend the book for both the depth of the research which it displays and the author's erudite presentation of the results. Hopefully, it will have a particular attribute - encouragement to other visiting or local authors to research and treat similarly another Forest village or town of his or her choice.

Cyril Hart
Coleford, Gloucestershire
April 1982

Preface to First Edition

This book started as a note on the back of an envelope to remind me, a 'foreigner' in the Forest, of a fragment of Parkend's history that I wanted to remember; and as I learned more about Parkend's fascinating past, I made more and more notes until I decided to put them in order and publish them in a book so that other people could readily share in my discoveries. If the book appears unbalanced, it is mainly because of the lack of information on some aspects and the embarrassing abundance of it on others. As research continued, some of the people in the story emerged from the shadows as interesting and amusing characters: canny John Morse, who ran the stampers for half a century but never appeared to prosper; the Rev. Henry Poole, worried about his school and striving, with the conscientious and public spirited deputy Surveyor, Edward Machen, to persuade the Office of Woods in London to give a little more money than they might otherwise be disposed to do; John James, who ran the ironworks for nearly 50 years, no doubt regretting that Machen lived on his doorstep, outwitting him when he could, but patiently dealing with all the correspondence that flowed between them; the first big coal master in Parkend, Edward Protheroe, with his many interlocking financial interests, and his clear distinction between charity and business; and the last coal master, Thomas Hedges Deakin, the archetypal late-Victorian businessman, who kept an iron grip on his empire until, at age 85, death forced him to relinquish it.

I should like to express my indebtedness to the authors of the books consulted. I should like also to thank Mr. G. Gibbs, Mr. A. K. Pope, Miss B. Griffith of Cinderford library and Robert Deakin, the Bishop of Tewkesbury, for permission to use photographs; Mr. H. W. Paar and Mr. A. E. Howell, the deputy Gaveller, for their assistance; Forest of Dean Newspapers Ltd for permission to consult their archives, the staff of the Dean Field Studies Centre, of the Coleford, Lydney and Gloucester public libraries and of the Gloucester and Kew Public Record Offices, for their courtesy and help; my wife for assisting in the research, sharing the field work and doing all the typing; and the many people who live in or have lived in Parkend for their friendliness, information and help.

Ralph Anstis
Parkend, Forest of Dean, Gloucestershire
May 1982

Preface to Second Edition

In this second edition the opportunity has been taken to make a few amendments and to introduce much new material, in particular more photographs. It is sad to record that the Parkend pound outside the turnpike house and the wharf at the Marsh Sidings have both been removed. Their disappearance shows that every effort must be made to preserve what remains of our 19th century heritage in Parkend.

My thanks go to Ian Pope, Anne Williams, Alan Powell and Harry Hook for additional information; Paul Griffiths, head teacher of Parkend School, for permission to use additional material about the school; Tony Wright for photographs from the Eric & Ann Gwynne collection; Bill Johns for various pictures; Dennis Parkhouse for the present day views; finally, the publishers for the use of material from the Parkhouse/Pope archive. I am also indebted to Michael Blackmore for the use of his drawing reproduced on page 14 and to Ian Pope for his realisation of the maps on pages 8 and 84/85.

Ralph Anstis
Coalway, Forest of Dean, Gloucestershire
September 1998

PARKEND. DEAN FOREST. FROM N.W. W.P. 504.

Parkend from York Lodge in about 1912. In the foreground are the roofs of Stampers Row. Smoke rises from the chimneys of the two terraces forming 'The Square' in the centre. To the right of them is the former ironworks engine house and in the distance Parkend Church can be seen.

Chapter 1
Then and Now

The story of Parkend in the Forest of Dean is not that of a pretty village with ancient church in sleepy churchyard overlooking a village green surrounded by timbered cottages and mentioned in Domesday. Famous writers and painters have not lived there. Nor have mediaeval kings and queens visited it. Parkend is none of this. It is not an old village: it did not exist two hundred years ago. It is, quite frankly, not a beautiful village, and visitors may be forgiven if they pass through it without appreciating that they have done so. For it has no clearly discernible centre. It straggles; there are no streets in the main part with houses on both sides. It does not centre round its church, which is on the outskirts of the village, hidden among the trees.

Yet if visitors stop and look round, they will find Parkend as satisfying as the standard picturesque village, if quite different. They will find an unusual phenomenon, shared it is true by a few other villages in the Forest, but an unusual phenomenon nevertheless. They will find that, beneath its rather uninteresting exterior, Parkend has an especially fascinating industrial history, mainly of the 19th century, but also dating back much earlier.

About 130 years ago Parkend was at its peak as an industrial village. The tide of industrialism that had engulfed Britain and brought her so much wealth and prestige as well as so much urban misery, had also lapped round Parkend and increased its size from a few scattered cottages to a sizeable industrial area. In the second half of the 19th century the village had a thriving ironworks, a tinplate works, two stoneworks, a wood sawmill, some stampers for crushing iron cinders and, within a radius of half a mile, a dozen coal mines. Trucks full of stone, wood, iron ore, cinders from the ironworks and coal were pulled by horses in a complex system of tramroads that criss-crossed the whole village. Railway trains steamed in and out and around. Coal and iron were loaded and unloaded at the dry Wharf. Parkend was busy, noisy and dirty.

Now all that bustle and noise have gone. The industrialism that created a large village from a few houses did not last long. In just over a hundred years it reached its climax and disappeared. Parkend's industries, its coal mines and its trams and trains have all gone. The big chimneys no longer send out their thick smoke. Gone, never to return, is the glimmer of lights in the miners' helmets as they came home from the pits through the trees, the sound of their boots going up the village street, and the sight of them on pay day squatting on one heel in groups of five or six outside the colliery company's offices, sharing out the group's earnings for the week. The coal tumps near the collieries no longer stand out from and scar the green of the Forest; they are now rounded green hills and merge in with the countryside. The tramroads are overgrown; some of the railway tracks, once so busy but now bereft of rails, have an air of unreal calm. However, all is not lost as the Dean Forest Railway has reintroduced passenger services to Parkend, the station has been rebuilt and the track relaid and it is thus possible to imagine, just briefly, the hustle and bustle of the station and the sound of steam locomotives from an age now gone.

Early Habitation

We shall never know when man first came to what we now call Parkend. The earliest date we know humans were there is about 300 AD for in 1852 over a thousand Roman coins were discovered near the present post office and village store, where the Parkend ironworks once stood. The coins were in a jar of common grey Roman pottery, which was broken by the finders to get at its contents. They were sold privately to two separate collectors. The oldest coin carries the image of the wife of Septimus Severus who died in 211 AD, and the newest that of Allectus the Usurper who was slain in 296 AD. There was only one silver coin in the find. The rest were all of small denominations, and this suggests that they were intended for paying the wages of labourers. Why would Romans or their British agents be paying labourers' wages in Parkend? What was the labour? Not iron ore mining, because there were no iron mines at Parkend. Perhaps coal mining, as there was some coal mining in Dean in Roman times. More likely it was charcoal making or iron smelting. Was there, perhaps, an iron furnace at Parkend at the end of the third century AD? If so, where did the labourers live? We do not know, and will probably never know the answers to these questions. Nor are we likely to discover whether anybody lived in the Parkend area during the following 1000 years.

The first house in Parkend was possibly the hunting lodge at Whitemead Park, which was built in the Middle Ages. Whitemead Park in those days was much larger than it is today, being about 300 acres in area. It was a deer park and extended southwards from Parkend over what is now called Parkhill Inclosure as far as Whitecroft bridge, and eastwards some distance over the present Lydney road (which did not exist until 1903), running up towards where the church is now. For centuries people have remarked on the hoarfrost that at times descends on Whitemead Park, and the name Whitemead may commemorate the fact that the area has long been a 'frost-hole'.

A new building replaced the mediaeval lodge in Queen Elizabeth I's reign; and a map of the Park (reproduced in part overleaf) shows that in 1776 it was divided into two farms, Thomas Barrows's on the west of the Cannop Brook (otherwise known as the River Lyd or the Newerne stream) and Sarah James's on the east. Barrows used the Lodge as his farmhouse. The northern part of his land spread westwards over to Parkend Bridge, which spanned the Cannop Brook, and still spans it. In Sarah James's farmland the map shows about ten coal pits marked 'coals have been got'. The Lodge was considerably extended in the late 18th and 19th centuries, when the grounds were laid out and a fish pond was created from the Darkhill brook which ran through them. It was burnt down in 1970 whilst being demolished.

If Whitemead Park Lodge was the first house in Parkend, we still have no idea when subsequent houses were built. In a document dated 1278 there is a reference to eight people who had eight charcoal pits at 'Wisgtemede', but this does not mean that they lived there or in the immediate vicinity. The first certainty of houses at Parkend is at the beginning of the 17th century when dwellings were built for some of

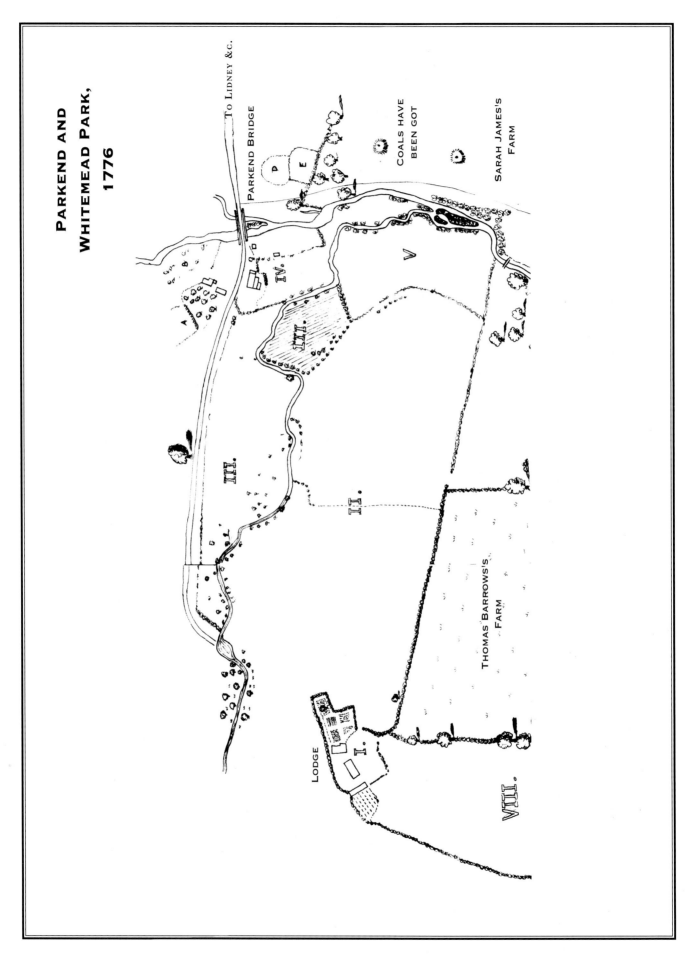

PARKEND AND WHITEMEAD PARK, 1776

To Lidney &c.

Parkend Bridge

D
E

Coals have been got

Sarah James's Farm

IV.

V

III.

III.

II.

Thomas Barrows's Farm

A

Lodge

I.

VIII.

the people employed in the King's ironworks which had just been erected there. So it is reasonable to take that time as the beginning of the tiny hamlet that was to have such an unusual history.

The hamlet could not have grown much in the next 200 years: indeed it may well have ceased to exist for a time. In the 18th century squatters probably moved into Parkend but even in 1799 when a new blast furnace was set up in the area, there could not have been more than a handful of inhabitants. Rudge, in his history of Gloucestershire dated 1803, does not list Parkend as a hamlet or even a 'place'. As late as 1833 a map was published with no reference to Parkend as a village, although Parkend bridge was marked.

In 1841, the earliest date for which it is possible to obtain a population figure, the number of inhabitants was only 78, and this was a time when the whole population of Britain was increasing rapidly, with the population of the Forest doubling between 1821 and 1841. In 1851 Parkend's population totalled 159, in 1861 it was 360 and in 1871, 583. By 1881 it had dropped to 542. In 1935 it was about the same, but by 1955 it had increased again to about 670. In 1981 it had dropped to about 540 and in 1997 it was down to around 450. The number of houses in Parkend in 1841 was 13, including Whitemead Park Lodge and the only other big house in the village, York Lodge. In 1859 the number was 76 (see Appendix 1): in 1881 it was 100.

Until the 20th century the name of the village was usually written as two words: Park End. It originally referred to the area at the end of Whitemead Park, since there is a reference in a document of 1616 to 'the ironworks at the Parke end'.

Much of the information in this book has been gleaned from *The Forest of Dean* by the Rev. H. G. Nicholls, published in 1858. Nicholls was vicar of Holy Trinity Church at Drybrook from 1847 to 1866, when he resigned because of ill health. He died the following year, aged 44. His book was the first general history of the Forest and it makes fascinating reading, especially in the chapters that give information about the early and mid-19th century. Not least interesting are the smaller items. Nicholls tell us, for example, that 'the finest of all the beeches in the Forest is near the entrance to Whitemead Park near York Lodge, measuring 17ft at 6ft from the ground'. Again, Nicholls tells us of an 'oak tree near York Lodge measuring 21ft round, formed apparently of two trees which grew together for ages, but not long since threatened to fall asunder, necessitating their being cramped up across the head by a transverse iron bar'.

An Oak near York Lodge. From Nicholls' *Forest of Dean*, **1858**

The Speech House in 1858

So we know that while Parkend as a village has existed for less than 200 years, people probably lived in the area for many years before. The life of these people in those distant days was no doubt similar to that of people in other parts of Dean.

The Forest has probably existed since about 8000 BC, although millions of years earlier there flourished the luxuriant forests that resulted in the coal that has lain and still lies under the Forest's surface. In the neolithic age the Forest probably covered about 100,000 acres. (Its present size is about 22,000 acres.) It filled the triangle formed by the River Wye in the west and the River Severn in the east, and stretched as far north as present-day Ross-on-Wye, Newent and Gloucester. In those days Parkend was in the very heart of the Forest, inaccessible, and most likely quite uninhabited. As local man slowly increased in numbers, he made incursions into the Forest perimeter and carved out settlements from the fringes of the woods. By the time the Romans arrived its area had been reduced to about 80,000 acres. After the Romans came the Anglo-Saxons, and the process of clearing the outer edges of the Forest continued. It seems that there were no people at Parkend in Saxon times because the area was still well inside the Forest. Lydney, Newnham, St Briavels, Staunton and Clearwell were settled at this time, but they were on the Forest edge.

Dean is a Royal Forest and has been since at least the time of King Canute at the beginning of the 11th century. In Norman times and later, the King's representative was the Constable of the Castle of St Briavels and Warden of the Forest of Dean. The office was honorary, and the officer actually in charge was the deputy constable. The Forest was administered from St Briavels Castle (built about 1130) until Crown offices were established in Whitemead Park in the 19th century. The Verderers' Court, which administered the laws about vert and venison (all vegetation and wild animals in the Forest), met at Kensley House in the centre of the Forest, and later at the Speech House which was built on the same site or nearby. Disputes were settled there, and offenders were brought there for preliminary examination. Minor offences were dealt with at Kensley House or the Speech House, but more serious cases were sent for trial before the Forest Justices at Gloucester. The Verderers' Court still meets several times a year at the Speech House.

There is no mention of Parkend in the Domesday Book (1086). Indeed, apart from intimating that there were iron mines, furnaces and small forges in the Forest, Domesday has little to say about the area. The Normans called it 'the Forest'. The land on the east, where Littledean, Mitcheldean and Abenhall now are, they called 'Dene', then 'Dean'. Later they applied the name to the woods as well. Denu in Anglo-Saxon means a hollow, and the word has survived in Shakespeare's Forest of Arden, West Dean in Sussex, and the Ardennes in France.

By the middle of the 13th century the Forest had shrunk to roughly its present size. All through the Middle Ages it was a wild place. William Camden wrote towards the end of the 16th century:

'This was a wonderful thicke Forest, and in former ages so darke and terrible, by reason of crooked and winding ways, as also the grisly shade therein, that it made the inhabitants more fierce, and bolder to commit robberies, for in the reign of Henry VI, they so infested all Severn Side with robbing and spoiling that there were lawes made by Parliament for to restrain them. But since that rich mines of iron were here found out, those thicke woods began to wax thin by little and little.'

In the 12th and 13th centuries the King was concerned to preserve the Forest as a hunting ground for himself and his court. Later, when he was less interested in hunting, he became more interested in exploiting it by using its wood in his various castles or for his ships, or simply by selling it. Later he made money by leasing areas to ironmasters for them to organise the mining, smelting and forging of iron. Consequently the King strove to keep the Forest intact, and tended to resist pressure to have areas hived off from the main body and turned into agricultural land.

As the centuries passed, the Crown relied more and more on the Forest to provide timber for the navy. The importance of Dean as a wood-producing area for the navy at the time of the Spanish Armada is shown by an entry in John Evelyn's diary. His informant was probably Samuel Pepys, who was a senior civil servant at the Admiralty. Evelyn wrote: 'I have heard that in the great expedition of 1588 it was expressly enjoined the Spanish Armada that if, when landed, they should not be able to subdue our nation and make good their conquest, they should yet be sure not to leave a tree standing in the Forest of Dean'.

Dean's great industry in the Middle Ages was iron making. Smelting in those days depended on charcoal which was made from Forest trees. While the Crown welcomed the income from the ironmasters, successive Kings were, in varying degrees, concerned to see that they did not use up the wood for charcoal at too quick a rate. The King was also concerned to see that the Foresters did not use too much wood for their houses and domestic fires and fences, and for their mines; and did not let their animals wander in the Forest in search of food and ruin the young trees. In fact, the story of the ordinary folk of Dean from the time of the Conquest, if not before, right up to the 19th century, is mainly that of a struggle to live off the land - they had little more than mining and animals – and to resist the acts of repression of both King and of those to whom he leased areas in the Forest.

Some Kings were more aware than others of the needs of their subjects to get a living, and granted the Foresters rights and privileges which, once obtained, they clung to jealously. Some of these privileges date from as early as the 12th century, and for hundreds of years afterwards they were disputed at times both by the King and by those to whom he had granted them. The privileges included estovers (the collecting of firewood and timber), pannage (the turning loose of swine in oak and beech woods in the autumn) and common and pasturage (the grazing of animals on common land). It is said that allowing sheep to graze in the Forest was a privilege granted by William the Conqueror to the Foresters in compensation for damage done by his deer and boars to the Foresters' holdings. However, these were privileges rather than rights. Today there are no longer any recognised privileges regarding estovers, although Forest Enterprise allows Foresters to collect firewood. Common and pannage in the unenclosed parts of the Forest, however, are now regulated.

A right that a Forester gained from the Crown and still has is the right to dig iron ore or coal in his own mine or to quarry stone as a free miner. Free mining rights applied originally to iron ore, but from the reign of Edward I (early 13th century) they applied equally to coal. In time Foresters also acquired certain rights to quarry stone. The free miners' rights were set out in a document called 'The Miners' Laws and Privileges', also known since the 19th century as the 'Book of Dennis'. It was probably compiled at the beginning of the 14th century, although the earliest known copy is dated 1610. This document states that the free miners' 'customes and franchises' were granted 'tyme out of minde'. It is thought that they date from the 13th century or even earlier. The rules and regulations under which free miners operate have been revised many times to suit changing circumstances. As defined in an Act of 1838, a Forester is a free miner if he is over 21 years old, was born in the Hundred of St. Briavels (nearly the same as being born in the Forest of Dean) and has worked a year and a day in a mine. This right entitles him to demand from the Gaveller a gale, that is an area of coal or iron ore, within the Hundred chosen by himself which he can dig, and the Gaveller is obliged to give him the gale, provided that a mine in the place chosen does not interfere with the working of any other mine. The miner pays a fee and his name is entered in the gale book. Though he is called a free miner, the gale holder must pay the Crown an annual rent and royalties on the minerals he removes from the ground. Free miners once enjoyed the right to take timber from the Forest for use in their mines; but after 1809 they could not do this if they used the tramroads; and the custom was finally done away with in 1838. After that date its value was taken into consideration when the rent of the gale, royalties and other charges were fixed. A free miner may work a gale himself, or do so in partnership with other free miners. He may also lease or sell his gale to someone who is not a free miner.

From early days coal and iron ore mining in Dean was regulated by the Court of Mine Law, which was supervised by the deputy Constables of St Briavels Castle and attended by the King's Gaveller or a deputy. This body, which may have derived from assemblies of free miners, consisted of 48 representatives chosen by free miners. The Court was quite a powerful body. Matters dealt with by it included fixing the selling price of coal, encroachment on other miners' gales, the fencing of pits to prevent accidents, and the collection of money for and the administration of a fund to provide financial aid to injured miners and for legal action taken on behalf of free miners. The Court also dealt with the ever-increasing problems caused by people from outside the Forest who wanted to mine there - foreigners, as they were called. In the early days Foresters had found that the conditions they had to satisfy before they could obtain a gale were sufficient to protect them from foreigners, but as coal mining became a growing industry some were tempted to sell or lease their mines to foreigners, who were richer than they were and able to develop the mines on a bigger scale than they could. Because of this, much bitterness arose between the free miners who were actively working their gales and the foreigners who had infiltrated into the coalfield. The Court last sat at the Speech House on 26 August 1777. A note attached to the last minutes of its proceedings stated that 'there has been no Court holden for the miners since this day, which is a great loss to the Gaveller, and causes various disputes amongst the colliers, which is owing to the neglect of the Deputy-Constables'. In fact, it seems that the officials refused to convene the Court any more on the grounds that it had become ineffective, a reason hotly denied by the free miners.

The Speech House was built in 1676 and considerably extended in the early 1880s. When this photograph was taken around 1905, it had been converted to a hotel but the old Verderers' Court Room was retained and now doubles as the dining room.

Chapter 3
The King's Ironworks at the Parke End

Iron ore was mined in Dean in prehistoric times. The ore was, and is, in a horseshoe shape on the edge of the coal deposits that lie under the centre of the Forest. Clearwell and Bream on the west, Wigpool and Edgehill on the east, were the principal mining areas. Prehistoric man had found the ore close to the surface and, since it was 70 per cent metal, he could work it. There is evidence that the iron ore mines at Lydney and Clearwell were being worked in pre-Roman times; and the scowles (quarries or mines) near Bream show that digging from the surface for the metal was a serious and relatively large-scale operation. In 1780 George Wyrrall, a Forest of Dean antiquarian, described the scowles as follows:

'There are, deep in the earth, vast concerns scooped out by men's hands and large as the aisles of churches; and on its surface are labyrinths worked among the rocks, and now long since overgrown with woods, which whosoever traces them must see with astonishment and incline to think them to have been the work of armies rather than private labourers.'

It does not seem that there was a great deal of mining and smelting before 200BC but from then onwards for hundreds of years these were the principal occupations in parts of Dean. To judge from the quantities of cinders they left behind, there must have been thousands of men employed in mining and smelting iron in Roman times. By the Middle Ages the Forest was the greatest iron working district in Britain. In 1282 there were at least 60 forges, although the number dropped to 45 two years later. These 60 forges required 900 charcoal pits to keep them going. The charcoal was made from wood and consequently the Forest was steadily eaten into, especially around Clearwell and Bream. The smelting was done where the necessary fuel could be found and, as the forges were moveable, when charcoal makers had used up the timber in one place they, and the smelters and their forges, could move to another. In the Middle Ages the taking of wood to make charcoal for iron making probably impoverished the Forest more than all other purposes put together.

In those days the ore was smelted by applying heat from charcoal by means of a shaft furnace. This process had probably been introduced by the Romans and was called the bloomery method. It was a simple one, which by no means extracted all the iron, and it needed little water. Enormous quantities of the cinders that remained after smelting were left around in the Forest unwanted for centuries. Later, when blast furnaces were available, the cinders were smelted again and yielded better quality iron than they had originally. As late as the beginning of the 19th century some 8,000 to 10,000 tons of cinders were lying at Parkend.

The bloomery system was replaced at the end of the 16th century by the blast furnace system. This was still fuelled by charcoal but needed much more of it than previously. It also required a good supply of water as the blast of air now necessary was provided by leather bellows driven by a waterwheel. The new emphasis on water power meant that the location of the furnace had to be near powerful and reliable streams and for the first time a good water supply nearby was more important than the location of ore, cinders, or wood for charcoal.

Blast furnaces came rather late to Dean. This was partly due to the conservatism of the free iron ore miners and their smelters, since they were in a position to exercise a monopoly in mining and smelting; and partly due to the Crown's unwillingness to allow the extra wood for the new process to be taken from the Forest when it might be used for shipbuilding. However, at the beginning of the 17th century the King, James I, was persuaded that there was money in the new system. He contracted with the Earl of Pembroke to set up four blast furnaces and three forges in the Forest. The Earl was to finance the enterprise and he commissioned Thomas Hacket, manager of the Company of Mineral and Battery Works, to build the furnaces and forges. Thus were the King's ironworks set up. To supply them with the necessary raw materials the King allowed the Earl to dig anywhere in the Forest for iron ore, coal and stone and to use cinders found anywhere there and to take an agreed amount of wood from it. No-one else was allowed to mine or take wood without the Earl's permission.

One of the furnaces and one of the forges were built at Parkend in 1612. The site of the furnace was most probably in the northern part of the area formed by the Cannop Brook, the lane that runs behind the *The Woodman* public house towards the lorry park and the lorry park itself. The furnace was 22ft high. As charcoal and iron ore were to be loaded into its top, it was necessary to have access at that level. The site chosen had a small hill some yards to the west of the brook and the gap between the hill and the furnace top was bridged by a wooden structure 12ft by 22ft which gave easy access to the top of the furnace. It was also used as a marshalling area for the raw materials. Part or all of the structure was covered over and was called the bridge-house. The blast for the furnace was provided by two pairs of leather bellows, about 15 to 20ft long and 5ft wide at the back, tapering to 2ft 6ins. at the front. The energy to move the bellows was supplied by a single waterwheel about 22ft in diameter. The water for the wheel came from a bay (or pool) at the head of 'a water course on the north side of the said furnace about half a mile long'. A second water course of the same length on the south side also fed into the bay. The course from the north was most likely the dry

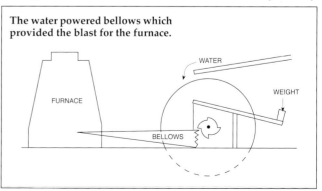

The water powered bellows which provided the blast for the furnace.

An artist's impression of a charcoal-fired blast furnace, with water driven bellows. This illustration by Michael Blackmore depicts the 17th century Llanelly Furnace, in the Clydach Gorge near Abergavenny, but the King's Furnace constructed at Parkend in 1612 would have been of very similar layout and appearance.

ditch (which can still be traced) that leaves the brook on its west side about 1,100 yards above the furnace site and runs south, bordering a Forest path during its last half mile or so. The course from the south was probably the ditch that within living memory ran from near International Timber's premises on the Coleford road to the furnace site. Water from these ditches was used 200 years later to work the wheel of a stamping mill (see page 41).

The exact site of the forge is not known but it was probably near the Cannop Brook, between the Blakeney road bridge and Parkend bridge. It did not need to back onto a hill but did require a large area for pools and waterways. By 1634 it was a double forge (having two hammers) with three fineries and a chaffery. In the finery the pig iron obtained from the furnace was refined, that is, decarburised and freed from impurities; and in the chaffery the refined iron was reheated, in order to be consolidated and shaped into bars by the hammers.

No sooner were the furnace and forge in operation than disputes erupted between the free miners and the ironmasters. When the King had granted the Earl of Pembroke the right to mine anywhere in the Forest, with no-one else allowed to do so without the Earl's permission, he had delivered a great blow to the free miners of Dean. Until then they had had the exclusive right to mine and this right was now taken away. The miners were determined not to accept the situation and clashes between them and the Earl's representatives resulted in a court case. The Court decided, on an interim basis, that existing miners could continue to take ore and cinders as a privilege but no new diggers were to be allowed, apart from 'such poor men as were inhabitants of the said Forest'. A final decision was not taken on the matter. The disturbances that had occurred, together with the knowledge that trees that could be used for making ships were being used to make charcoal, led

to the King suspending the operation of the ironworks the same year as, or the year after, they were opened. Anxious as he was to make money from the ironmasters he was, as ever, concerned about the consumption of wood. However, he was soon in need of more revenue so he tried again and in May 1615 he leased the works to Sir Basil Brooke of Shropshire who was in partnership with Richard Chaldecott of London.

In 1618, mainly because of Brooke's illegal felling of trees, the King suspended the ironworks again but in April 1621 he leased them once more, this time for seven years to Richard Challoner and Philip Harris. When the lease ran out Pembroke again obtained the concession (this time for 21 years) and sublet to Sir Basil Brooke, George Mynne and Thomas Hackett.

In the 1630s Dean was supporting about eleven blast furnaces and eleven forges (of which four furnaces and five forges were owned by the Crown) as well as privately owned works close to but outside the Forest. This concentration of ironworks was probably greater than anywhere else in the country.

In 1635 the King's ironworks in the Forest were surveyed. In Parkend it was found that the furnace needed to have about £60 spent on it to put it in good shape, and the double forge £25. The survey tells us that the furnace itself was 22ft square at the bottom. The furnace house (the casting house where the molten metal ran out of the furnace into the sand where it set) was 'built with stone, 22ft square and 9ft high in the side-walls, the roof good except one little breach by the bridge, and tiled'. The bridge-house was '42ft long, 22ft broad, the side-walls 8ft 6in. high, covered with boards, double bottomed with planks upon strong sleepers, with fence walls, and in repair'. The hutch, a wide drain below the waterwheel to carry away the water after it had turned the wheel, was 6ft deep, 3ft broad and 70ft long.

Usually a hutch was covered, but here it was not and to keep rubbish and earth out planks had been laid across it. All was in repair but the stream was 'stopped [choked] below the hutch with cinders'. There were also troughs 'cut out of sound timber covered with planks', and a pent-house under the furnace – not a warm luxury flat for the manager, but a chamber built underneath the bottom stone of the furnace to collect ground moisture. Other buildings at the furnace were: a cabin for the bridge-server 18ft long and 11ft broad, built of timber and covered with boards; a cabin adjoining the furnace for the furnace keeper; a fair house three storeys high, tiled, the ends built with stone and the rest with timber, 50ft long, 16ft broad, with two stables of timber belonging thereto; the founder's house and a cottage adjoining; and a 'small cottage now enjoyed by William Wayte'.

The survey also gave details of the forge and its waterways. There was a bay, whose lower part was 120ft long, and a wooden floodgate with six sluices. These opened onto 160ft of water which was confined by stone walls 3ft high and 3ft thick. Part of this area was 'aproned and planked on the top for a bridge'. There were also two troughs, one 32ft and the other 66ft long, the latter leading to the finery. Other buildings included a small carpenter's shed; a storehouse for iron, 24ft by 18ft and 13ft high in the sidewalls, built in stone and timber and tiled; two coalhouses, one of which was 62ft by 29ft and 17ft high in the sidewalls, built in stone and timber; a coal yard 50ft in circumference with an 8ft wall; a four-roomed stone house for the coal keeper which was tiled; a smaller house for the finer which was 'covered with boards'; a house for the hammerman; and 'two cottages enjoyed by the finers'.

In the year 1640 the King – now Charles I – took the greatest single action any monarch has taken against the interests of the Forest. As a consequence of his growing quarrel with Parliament he was short of money. To help correct this situation he required the lessees of his ironworks to surrender their lease, and then leased 17,000 to 18,000 acres of the Forest, practically the whole of it, to Sir John Wyntour. Included in the arrangements were the ironworks, cinders and timber (except as ever, trees that could be used for building ships), and the iron ore, coal and stone beneath the surface. Wyntour was Secretary to the Queen, Henrietta Maria, but he was also an acute businessman who had ironworks at Lydney. The transaction was, in effect, a sale. Wyntour paid £106,000 and an annual fee-farm rent of £1,950 12s. 8d. for the concession. He was now the greatest ironmaster in England.

Wyntour began to demolish the Forest. The Foresters soon saw that their livelihood was disappearing and protested strongly. They petitioned the King for their rights and privileges to be protected and before long there was litigation involving them, Wyntour and the Crown. In March 1642 the House of Commons voted for ending Wyntour's concession. The Civil War now erupted. The backlash of it swirled round Parkend and in 1644 the furnace and forge were destroyed. When the King was beaten, Cromwell took away Wyntour's estates and concessions in Dean. An attempt at re-afforestation was made but because this meant enclosing land the Foresters resisted it.

After the execution of Charles I in 1649, a Commission was appointed by the Government to report on the state of the Forest and in particular on the abuses that had occurred since 1641. The Commission recommended that, because of the enormous amounts of wood being used, all the ironworks in the Forest should be destroyed; otherwise the State would be forced to send abroad for ship timber. As a result, Parliament ordered the demolition of the ironworks.

However, as we know, Governments can quickly change their mind. In 1653 a Major John Wade was appointed as the Government's chief administrator in Dean. He was instructed to build another iron furnace at Parkend to replace the one destroyed in the Civil War and to manufacture iron shot, cannons and guns. This new furnace was probably about the same size as the earlier one but stood a short distance further downstream. Wade planned for a greater volume of water 'to move the bellows' and said that his new Parkend furnace would be 'one of the best watered furnaces in this nation'. Wade also erected at Whitecroft, lower down the Cannop Brook, a forge to convert into shot and ordnance the raw iron produced at Parkend. The new furnace began operating in 1654 and for six years large quantities of pig iron, shot and ironware were produced. From 1654 to 1659 Wade supplied the navy with 700 tons of shot and 88 tons of wrought-iron fittings. In 1655 he informed the Admiralty that if sufficient shot had been made, he wished to 'turn the furnaces so as to cast pig iron' and between 1657 and 1660 he produced some 1,200 tons of pig iron and 300 to 400 tons of bar iron.

After the restoration of the monarchy in 1660, the new King, Charles II, appointed Wm. Carpenter, Philip Rod and George Wyrrall to work the Parkend and other Crown ironworks for him. He also granted much of the Forest to Wyntour again, who thereupon resumed his demolition of it.

A Commission was now appointed to report on the running of the King's ironworks. In 1662 it reported that the Parkend furnace, though excellent, needed 'a roof to the colehouse and some other repairs', which might cost about £40. ('Cole' was charcoal; what we call coal was then called sea-coal.) More importantly, the Commission urged the King to run the Parkend works and the Whitecroft forge himself because by so doing they would be more profitable to him since he would be able to provide the navy with iron at a cheaper rate than he was currently paying. But the King decided not to accept this advice and from 1662 leased them to some nominees of Wyntour's, Francis Finch and Robert Clayton, for 11 years. One of the first things Finch and Clayton did was to rebuild the forge at Parkend which had, like the furnace, been destroyed during the Civil War. The rebuilt forge was in use from 1662 to 1674. Finch and Clayton did not hold the lease long. Trouble broke out with the Foresters about rights to graze animals in the areas where the ironworks were operating and Wyntour was felling more trees than his contract allowed. So in 1667 the King terminated the lease of the ironworks and took Wyntour's concessions away. By then the Forest had been practically destroyed. Of over 30,000 trees, only 200 were left. Strange that an Englishman had managed to do what the Spanish Armada could not!

The King now decided once and for all that the conservation of the Forest was more important than the income from his ironworks and in 1674 the Parkend furnace and forge, the Whitecroft forge and all the other Crown ironworks in Dean, including all buildings and employees' houses, were sold for demolition to a Mr. Paul Foley for £500. And that was the end – after 62 years – of the King's ironworks at Parkend.

The ironworks were destroyed but some evidence was left of their previous existence. David Mushet, the famous metallurgist and ironmaster of the l9th century, wrote that in about 1812 he saw the ruins of Parkend furnace. They were 'surrounded by a large heap of slag or scoria that is produced in making pig iron. As the situation of this furnace was remote from roads, and must at one time have been deemed nearly inaccessible, it had all the appearance at the time of my survey of having remained in the same state for nearly two centuries. There existed no trace of any sort of machinery; which rendered it highly probable that no part of the slags had been ground (the usual practice) and carried off, but that the entire produce of the furnace in slags remained undisturbed. The quantity of slags I computed at from 8,000 to 10,000 tons'.

A few years after Mushet's visit a stamping mill was set up nearby and the slag he had found was used up; but a little still remains under the grass to remind us of where the King's ironworks had been. Part of the area is now a copse through which the Cannop Brook runs. As it passes through the trees it splits into several separate streams, the result perhaps of damming to provide the pools necessary to run the furnace. A path leading into the copse goes nowhere and this delightful spot is probably never visited nowadays, except by the occasional industrial archaeologist and, perhaps, small boys on voyages of exploration.

If the King had controlled the use of timber more closely and had insisted on a programme of tree replacement by systematic enclosure, the King's ironworks might have continued and benefited the inhabitants of Parkend longer. As John Evelyn said in 1663: 'Nature has thought fit to produce the wasting ore more plentifully in woodland than any other ground, and to enrich our forests to their own destruction'.

The copse behind the stamping mill. The bridge probably once carried a tramroad.

Chapter 4
The Forest and the Foresters from 1675

After Wyntour had ruined the Forest, an effort was made to restock it with trees; but first it was decided to reorganise the Forest administration. An Act of Parliament was passed in 1668 setting out the new arrangements and in the following years they were put into effect. In 1676 the Speech House was built, replacing Kensley House. The Verderers' Court had sat there and continued to sit at the new Speech House, which was from now on to be the administrative centre of more of the business of the Forest. From 1680 most of the sittings of the Court of Mine Law were held there. In 1675 the bounds of the Forest were revised, and they have remained much the same to this day. The Forest itself was divided into six walks, in place of the ten bailiwicks that had until then existed. Each walk had a keeper, who was provided with a lodge to which was attached 30 acres of ground. The Parkend area, which had previously been in the bailiwick of Staunton, was now placed in the York Walk, named after the King's brother, the Duke of York. Later the walk was also known as Parkend Walk. The boundary of the walk ran from where the King's ironworks had been, along the Brookhall Ditches stream to Yorkley Wall, through Yorkley, Kidnalls, Whitecroft, Brockhollands, Ellwood, Bream, Bream Cross, Poolway Lane End, Bixhead Slad, along the Cannop Brook and then back to the King's ironworks. York Lodge on the northwest side of the village was formerly the house occupied by the managers of the King's ironworks. It was probably the most important of the lodges, as it was the head keeper's. It was destroyed in 1688 but was rebuilt shortly after. Today little of the original structure remains. By 1859 it was being leased to private individuals. It is said that the song 'Little Brown Jug' was composed there.

Near the Lodge a small building was built as the venison store for the whole Forest. It is still there but is roofless and rapidly decaying, the fact that it has been scheduled as a protected building hardly compensates for its sorry state.

One of the more important provisions of the 1668 Act empowered the Crown to enclose up to 11,000 acres of the Forest for the purpose of growing timber. In enclosed areas Foresters lost their rights and privileges to graze animals and take wood. In this way, by changing the areas enclosed when the young trees were big enough to stand up against the Foresters and their animals, the Forest administrators could ensure that there was always a substantial area of the Forest protected. Unfortunately it was a long time before the maximum acreage of 11,000 (which still obtains) was reached.

Enclosing areas where the Foresters had previously grazed their animals and taken wood and game triggered off serious disorders. In 1688 York Lodge was pulled down by irate Foresters from the Parkend area. The Speech House was also damaged. When the Foresters' animals were found in the new enclosures, Crown officials put them in pounds, and the Foresters had to pay a fine to retrieve them. This new policy was not, of course, popular. Most of the Foresters concerned had nowhere else to keep the animals, so they were turned loose in the Forest until they were impounded again. One of the four pounds in the Forest was at Parkend along the Coleford Road on the right, almost opposite the old turnpike house at the Bream turning. It was removed in 1985. The following appeared in the *Gloucester Journal* on 22 July 1735:

'Whereas a notorious and villainous gang of persons have several times of late assembled themselves together in a riotous manner and committed divers disorders by breaking open the pounds at the Castle of St. Briavels and Parkend Lodge and discharged from thence several cattle. And upon Saturday night the 5th instant, the same gang came to the lodge of Mr. R. Worgan [a local landowner and probably the guardian of the pound], entered his garden, beat down his beans, cut up his cabbages and apple trees, broke his windows and part of the pound wall; then adjoined to the Speech House Lodge where they did more damage.'

Discontent and poverty among the Foresters continued during most of the 18th century. A report in about 1780 said that the persons living in the Forest were 'chiefly poor labouring people who are inclined to seek habitation [there] for the advantage of living rent free and having the benefit of pasturage for a cow or a few sheep and of keeping pigs in the woods'. Most of these squatters were from neighbouring parishes but some were foreigners from other parts of Britain, especially Wales.

In 1795 came the Bread Riots. The Foresters were accustomed to barter their produce for corn for their bread with farmers on the Forest edge. During the Napoleonic war, this corn was bought up by the Government for the army and navy and very little, if any, was available for the Foresters. One day in 1795 some Foresters hijacked two wagons loaded with barley and wheat which were on their way to Gloucester market and the next Saturday there was a more serious incident at Ross which ended with the military being called in. There were also disturbances at Awre. Because of the scarcity of grain and its high price, the Government deemed it prudent to distribute £1,000 worth of grain among the distressed Foresters.

At the same time, as if to worsen the poverty, the Government was still trying, with varying success, to prevent Foresters from taking wood unlawfully. A public notice was put on display in 1791 by the Surveyor General of His Majesty's Woods and Forests, setting out the penalties for doing this in Royal Forests. It is a very long document, phrased in the impressive literary English of the time, which most contemporary Foresters must have found incomprehensible even if they could read it. It starts grandly:

'Great Depredations and Abuses having been committed, in lopping, topping, damaging, spoiling and cutting down, and carrying off, without Assignment of His Majesty's Officers, divers Trees, and Trees likely to become Timber Trees, and Quantities of Wood, Underwood, Poles, Young Trees, Sticks of Wood, Green Stubs, Hollies, Thorns, Quicksets, Hedgewood and Bushes ...'

It continues for another 1,300 words in similar vein setting out the penalties for such felonious actions. If caught, the felon was fined, sent to the Common Gaol, 'committed to the House of Correction to hard labour and publicly whipped once a month on a Market-Day between the Hours of Eleven and Two ... deemed to be an incorrigeable rogue and punished as such' or transported for seven years.

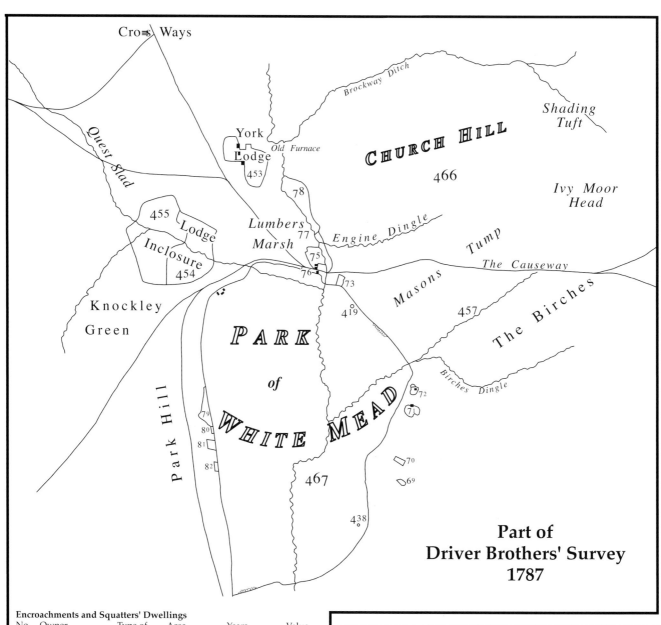

Part of
**Driver Brothers' Survey
1787**

Encroachments and Squatters' Dwellings

No.	Owner	Type of Cottage	Area a-r-p	Years encroached	Value £.s.d.
69	Warren James	Turf	0-1-26	5	0.15.0.
70	" "				
71	Jeptha James	Turf	0-2-15	7	0.18.0.
72	Jonathan Perkins	Turf	0-1-4	4	0.6.0.
73	James Keer		0-1-0	7	0.3.0.
75	" "		1-1-24	40	0.12.0.
76 } 77 } 78 }	" "		2-0-4 3-1-34	20 }	3.10.0.
79	" "		1-1-16	40	0.12.0.
80	Richard Williams		0-2-4	2	0.7.6.
81 } 82 }	James Prichard		0-0-21	4 }	0.2.6.

Properties

No.	Owner	Property	Area a-r-p
453	Robert East	The Keepers Lodge	5-3-15
454		Meadow	12-0-25
455		Rough Ground	16-0-11
457			174-3-30
466			206-2-0
467	White Mead Park		234-1-30

Coal Pits

419 Isaac Kear
438 Lord Sherborne & Co.

Edward Machen (1783-1862), Deputy Surveyor of Dean 1808-1854.

Such a notice seems amusing now but its purpose was the opposite and must have been regarded by the Foresters as another attack on what they considered their right to gain a living in the Forest. There is no doubt that their poverty was considerable. A report in 1810 said that they were in a condition 'nearly as wretched as anything now existing in Ireland'. The same report, however, gave a less than sympathetic view of the Foresters' personality. They were, it said, 'exceedingly excitable, perpetually at strife amongst themselves, so jealous of any 'foreigners' coming into the Forest as to deter most persons, highly suspicious of any effort to improve the property of the Crown, even when intended for their personal good, repeatedly destroying the new plantations and terrifying the adjoining districts by forming riotous mobs'.

The Napoleonic wars had drawn attention to Britain's dependency on good oak for her ships. Lord Nelson visited Dean in 1802 and was perturbed by the state of the Forest and its deficiencies in timber-trees. In his opinion the poor state of the Forest was due, among other things, to official inattention. 'Vast droves of hogs are allowed to go into the woods in the autumn, and if any fortunate acorn escapes their search, and takes root, then flocks of sheep are allowed to go into the Forest, and they bite off the tender shoot ... There is also another cause of failure of timber: a set of people called Forest Free Miners, who consider themselves as having a right to dig for coal in any part they please'.

As a result of reports such as this, further efforts were made to grow timber. Whitemead Park had been leased to successive Earls of Berkeley since the end of the 17th century and sublet by them to farmers. In 1808 the Surveyor General of Woods and Forests refused to renew the lease on the grounds that the Park was unfavourably situated for farming purposes and the buildings on it were in very bad repair. Noting that some excellent timber was growing on the land, he decided to have the whole area planted with oak. In 1816 the lodge was refurbished as the deputy Surveyor's office and residence. It was used for this dual purpose up to 1969, when the last deputy Surveyor to live and work in Dean, Mr. R. G. Sanzen-Baker, retired. In that year the deputy surveyor's office in Dean was moved to Coleford.

In 1810 the office of Surveyor General of Woods and Forests was replaced by that of the Commissioners of Woods, Forests and Land Revenues of the Crown. The department was known as the Office of Woods for short, and their local representative in the Forest was the deputy Surveyor. Edward Machen held this post from 1808 to 1854, and was consequently Parkend's most important inhabitant during most of those years. He died in 1862, aged 79. His ancestors had lived in Dean from the middle of the 17th century, and many had held posts connected with the Forest. His father had been deputy Surveyor General (and deputy Gaveller) and Edward succeeded him in these posts. He was a conscientious servant of the Crown, writing detailed accounts of matters that arose from his day-to-day administration that still make interesting reading today. Machen was a religious man who regularly worshipped at Parkend Church, where he took a boys' Sunday school class. According to the Rev. H. G. Nicholls he was one day teaching the class about being 'inheritors of the Kingdom of Heaven. He asked, "And how, my boys, are you to get it for your own?" "I takes it in" was the reply, in allusion to the mode of possession commonly practised by Foresters when anxious to augment their territory'.

In 1818 Machen reported that the saplings planted in Whitemead Park ten years earlier were 'thriving very well in all parts which are situated at a distance from the brook, but near it they are very thin and stunted and unhealthy and are constantly killed down by spring frosts'. Machen

Whitemead Park, office and residence of the deputy Surveyor, the Crown's chief administrator in Dean from 1816 to 1969, when the house was demolished. The grounds are now used by the Civil Service Motoring Association as a leisure park.

also stated that most of the 'large timber now in the Forest is about Parkend on Church Hill, Ivy Moor Head, Park End Lodge Hill, Russell's Inclosure and at the Lea Bailey ... The timber at Parkend is very fine, and I should suppose from 150 to 200 years old', i.e. planted between 1620 and 1670. On 29 May 1819, according to Machen, the frost was so severe that the verdure around Whitemead Park was entirely destroyed. There was not a green leaf left on any oak or beech, large or small, and all that year's shoots had withered. However, by August the trees had made more shoots and the plantations had recovered. There were severe frosts again in the next two years, one as late as 23 June.

A Notable Visitor

In August 1823 the Duke of Wellington paid a short visit to Whitemead Park. He was invited over from Cheltenham by his friend Charles Arbuthnot. Arbuthnot, who had been appointed a Commissioner of Woods a few months earlier, had come down to Dean on official business and was stopping with Machen at Whitemead Park. The Duke rode over early one morning, took breakfast with Arbuthnot and Machen and spent the day in Dean. At 5 am the next morning he rode back to Cheltenham. Thus did Parkend's most illustrious visitor come and go within 24 hours!

Foresters' Unrest

All through the first part of the 19th century unrest continued in the Forest. Foreigners and enclosures were the principal causes. Free miners were becoming more and more hostile to the foreigners who were coming to Dean and taking over the mines, and all Foresters were becoming restive about the Government's policy on enclosures, which kept them and their animals out of parts of the Forest. Machen recorded that 'in May 1831 several of the single trees planted near Park End and on Bream's Eaves were wilfully cut off in the night and no discovery made of the offenders'. Shortly after, he reported that gates of plantations had been broken open and Foresters had driven their animals into the forbidden areas, and that part of the wall on Oaken Hill Inclosure had been destroyed. These were signs of a storm that was soon to break. The unrest was headed by a man called Warren James, who was born between Parkend and Whitecroft.

In June 1831 Warren James called on the Foresters to destroy all the enclosure walls and fences in Dean as a protest against the poverty and unemployment that the arrival of foreigners in Dean and the exclusion of their animals from the newly enclosed areas had caused. The Foresters began with the destruction of the walls of the Park Hill Inclosure, which was on the Whitecroft side of Parkend, and they then turned to other enclosure walls. They continued for several days and soon nearly 2,000 people, including women and children, had joined in the destruction. The militia was called out from Monmouth but it consisted mainly of old men and boys and did not succeed in quelling the riots, so dragoons were brought in from Merthyr Tydfil, where they had just repressed some riots. The Forest was put under martial law, the ringleaders were arrested and the Foresters dispersed. By now scarcely a mile of unbroken walls or fences remained anywhere in the Forest. Warren James was caught hiding in a coal pit in Bream and after trial was sentenced to death. This was subsequently changed to transportation for life. The others were given up to two years imprisonment.

Living and Working Conditions

The quelling of the riots by force did nothing to alleviate the poor living conditions of the Foresters. Nor were matters improved by the rapid increase in population and the influx of workers into the mines and other industrial concerns that was taking place at this time. Conditions of work in the mines and factories were poor and remained quite unacceptable by present standards until the 20th century. There was no legislation controlling conditions of work in mines in Dean or anywhere else in Britain until 1842. In 1840 the Government appointed a Commission to look into the employment of children in mines and factories. The Commission reported that parents were forced by poverty to send their children out to work and that they were encouraged to do so by the great demand by employers for child labour. The Commission found that in nearly every district in Britain children were employed underground in mines at the age of six, in some cases at five or even younger. These child workers pulled trucks of coal along underground passages too narrow for grown men, or looked after ventilating doors under conditions that were very like solitary confinement in darkness. The Commission reported that Dean Forest children were employed as such door-boys. They began to work in the mines as young as six or seven, earning three shillings (15p) a week. Forty of the 700 miners employed in the Bilson pit were under the age of thirteen. The Commission also found Dean children working in the ironworks. Twenty of the 100 workers at Cinderford ironworks were between the ages of nine and thirteen, and all did regular night and Sunday work.

Women also worked in Forest mines, dragging and carrying coal; and Timothy Mountjoy, a Forest collier, said in 1887 that in the 1820s and 1830s he 'had seen lots of Forest of Dean women at work winding up the coal out of shallow pits ten and twelve, and sometimes fifteen and twenty-five, yards deep. They also loaded it into carts and donkeys' and mules' bags ... These women had to be at their posts like men in all weathers'.

As a result of the Commission's report the Mines and Quarries Act of 1842 was passed which prohibited the employment underground of women and of children under the age of ten. This was a start, and further legislation followed slowly. It was not until 1864 that legislation about conditions of employment covered all types of factory, including foundries and blast furnaces. For many boy miners working conditions remained poor until the mines closed in the 20th century. One of the owners of Trafalgar Colliery in evidence before a Select Committee in 1874 said that some seams worked in his colliery were only 17 inches deep; and as late as the 1920s boys of 13 pulled loads of coal at the New Fancy Colliery, sometimes through water, along tunnels not much deeper.

There is no reason to believe that employment conditions in the 19th century were better in Parkend than elsewhere in Dean, that Parkend children did not, as a matter of course, work long hours down the pits and in the ironworks. There is no reason either to suppose that employers in Dean were any more benevolent towards their workers than those in other parts of the country. These were the days of *laissez faire*, when the people in control believed that it was best for society if everyone was free to follow his own 'enlightened self-interest'. With this approach most employers and shareholders managed very well and lived comfortably; but the workers in mines and factories did less well. A prospectus dated 1852 for the formation of the Park End Colliery Company put the situation in a nut-shell. The prospectus stated that the cost of raising coal from the Parkend and New Fancy collieries and conveying it to Lydney was amply covered by 7s. 1d. (35p) a ton. The selling price in Lydney was 12s. (60p) a ton. If only 100,000 tons of coal were raised a year, after deduction of all management expenses a dividend of 25 per cent could be paid to the shareholders. (This, at a time when there was little or no inflation.) But, the prospectus went on, the demand for coal was growing, and if more pits were opened and more coal dug, the profits could go even higher. Adult miners were earning about 3/- (15p) a day in those days. Low wages were clearly a prerequisite of high dividends.

Improvements in working conditions as the century progressed, slow as they were in coming, did reduce the misery of the working people in Dean and the sporadic outbursts of violence that it engendered. The introduction of churches and schools in the central part of the Forest has been advanced as another reason for the decrease in unrest and violence.

Parkend Church

Parkend had no church until 1822. Before then Forest people were considered for religious purposes to belong to the parish of Newland – but they rarely went to any of the churches in that parish. The vicar of Newland, writing in 1819, said that in 1803, when he had become vicar, the language of the Foresters 'was most deplorable – habitual profanation of the Sabbath-day, drunkenness, rioting, immodest dancing, revellings, fightings, an improper state of females on their marriage, and an absence and ignorance of the Holy scriptures'. The vicar and others worked hard to remedy the situation, and by 1817 churches had been built at Berry Hill and Drybrook. It was considered that when one was built at Parkend all Foresters would have reasonable access to a church. The Rev. Henry Poole appealed in 1819 for public aid towards the erection of a church and school house there. The money was found and the Office of Woods gave five acres of land on Mason's Tump for the buildings. The Severn & Wye Railway & Canal company provided a special tramroad siding to the site and conveyed the Forest stone for the church free of charge. The church was designed by the Rev. Poole, who had been an architect in Bristol before coming to Dean, and cost £2,731. It was dedicated as the Church of St. Paul on 2 May 1822 by the Lord Bishop of Gloucester. Though designed to seat 500, over 1,000 people crammed into it for the dedication service and many who could not gain admission clung to the bars of the windows on the outside. The Rev. Poole was its first vicar; his discourses, according to Nicholls, 'were persuasively delivered, earnest in character and composed in an engaging style'.

The site of the church seems nowadays to be an unsuitable one, since it is not in the village and is not even on a road that leads anywhere. Its location was, in fact, carefully chosen. In the 1820s Parkend was no more than a scattering of a few houses with a population of two or three dozen. The church was not intended for Parkend alone but for a population of 400, mainly at Whitecroft, Pillowell, Yorkley, Ellwood and Moseley Green. Further, while the church is not now on a road going anywhere, in those days it was on a path to Whitecroft, Pillowell and Yorkley (the present Parkend to Whitecroft road was not built until over 80 years later).

St. Paul's Church, Parkend, about 1858. It was built in 1822 and the ecclesiastical parish was constituted in 1844 under an Act of 1842. The parish originally extended from Blakeney Hill to Clearwell Meend and from the Speech House to Coalway but its area was considerably reduced in 1854, 1856, and 1866.

Parkend Parsonage and School

In addition to a site for the church, there was, Nicholls tells us, also enough land for the erection of 'a picturesque parsonage and also commodious schools'. The parsonage was not completed for some years; when the Rev. Poole moved into it in 1829 it was still not finished.

The 'schools' were in fact one school. It was a National School designed to take about 200 children. There were many such schools in England in those days when there was no national system of state education. They were established by the National Society for the Education of the Poor according to the principles of the Church of England, and were maintained by donations from local people and organisations and pennies from the children who attended. In Parkend 'on account of the poverty of the neighbourhood' only £15 a year was to be expected from individual donations and £15 from the children.

In March 1822 the vicar suggested to Machen that the school should be built on a site south-east of the church, which would be especially convenient for children walking through the Forest from Whitecroft and Yorkley. The Office of Woods would not agree to this site because they thought that the children would injure the trees on their way to and from school, and it was finally built in 1822 on the Yorkley road at the end of the vicarage drive. The National Society gave £200 towards its construction.

When the vicar had raised the question of a site for the school he had also asked if a cottage could be built at the end of the vicarage drive. There was a gate there, but to keep it locked all the time would be inconvenient to visitors, and to leave it open would subject the vicarage and grounds to 'intrusions and depredations'. He proposed that the cottage 'should be always and solely for the accommodation of a servant connected with the church or school, a clerk, a schoolmaster or sexton' so that such intrusions and depredations could be prevented. The provision of a cottage was agreed by the Office of Woods, and it was built in 1824 on the west side of the drive, opposite the school. The cottage, which is still there, was for the occupation of the schoolmaster and mistress. The Office of Woods contributed towards the cost of its erection, and also contributed annually towards its maintenance and to the master's and mistress's salary (£40 a year).

So the school was not where the vicar had wanted it, and its inauspicious beginning presaged difficulties for at least the first

St. Paul's, Parkend sits on top of Mason's Tump and was dedicated in May 1822. When originally built the church served a wide area of the Forest, its congregation traversing a network of paths through the woodlands.

A closer view of the south side of the church showing the unusual octagonal nave and buttresses. In the background can be seen the vicarage.

Parkend Church about 1910, with part of the graveyard visible. Here will be found the tomb of the Rev. Henry Poole the first vicar and the architect of the church.

The interior of St. Paul's church, also taken around 1910, showing the spaciousness afforded by the octagonal nave with no supporting pillars. Note the ornate gas lamps on either side.

60 years of its life. In 1842 the school had to be closed because it was unsafe. In about 1835 cracks had begun to appear in the walls of the building, and the ground around it had begun to sink. The cause was subsidence, the result of activities in Mr. Protheroe's nearby colliery. The vicar tackled Mr. Protheroe on the matter, but the latter doubted whether it could be proved that the damage had been caused by his mine and refused to do anything about it. So in March 1843 the vicar told Machen the sad story, and suggested that the only remedy was to build a new school in a new place. Machen espoused the cause and wrote to the Commissioners of Woods in London. He told of the cracks in the walls which, he said, for the last five years had 'from time to time got out of the perpendicular … Now it is considered by most persons who have viewed it to be unsafe for a school. Others, however, and especially Mr. Protheroe's agent, say that the building may stand many years and that in mining districts men constantly live in houses in a more apparently dangerous state'. Mr. Machen added that there was no doubt that 'the school has been undermined by Mr. Protheroe's works'.

The Commissioners agreed to provide the school with 'a different site affording more secure foundations'. In the event, for reasons that cannot be discovered, it was rebuilt on the same site as the old one. The Office of Woods contributed £115 and the National Society £50 towards the cost. The rebuilt school was opened in 1845. Like the old school it was 40ft square, and had two windows on each of the four sides. Projecting from the side facing the road were two closets, one for 'hats etc.' and the other for 'bonnets etc.', and on each side was an entrance. The inside was divided down the middle from north to south. Each half had a fire-place, and the master's and mistress's desks were close to their respective fires.

Parkend school also served pupils from the Viney Hill and Blakeney areas until the early 1850s when schools were opened there. From then onwards the three schools were governed by one Committee run by the vicar. The Committee members usually included the deputy Surveyor and several local industrialists.

In January 1855 the indefatigable vicar approached Machen about reorganising and refitting the school. The cost would be £60 but, as the Committee of the Council on Education were putting up £40, he asked for only £20. He said that the school was 'not so efficient as it ought to have been, it being an old school building, and not fitted up to suit modern acquirements'. This, when the school had supposedly been completely rebuilt only ten years previously! Machen passed the request for £20 to the Commissioners in London.

The school was indeed not so efficient as it ought to have been. The schoolmaster was, we learn, 'unfitted for his situation' and unpopular with the children. Their attendances had dropped and so had their contributions. Then the master had left and the school had closed. In the opinion of one Parkender, Mr Peter Jenkins of Birch Cottage, the situation was extremely bad. He wrote to the Commissioners: 'Although far from joining in the popular outcry as to the management of the Royal Forests, yet I confess that I think the same susceptible of improvement and as an instance I beg to quote the notorious case of Parkend school which has long received £30 per annum from H.M. Government and yet from its isolated position, the frequent long periods it has been closed and other causes it would be invidious to mention, it has ever been all but quite useless to the Forest, and the case seems still worse under the present auspices, for the

Parkend School about 1912. On the right is the house where the schoolmaster and schoolmistress lived.

school has never been opened during the present year'. The Commissioners asked for Whitemead Park's comments on the letter. Sir James Campbell, who had now succeeded Edward Machen as deputy Surveyor, had to admit that the school was not going as well as it might - indeed it had been closed for nine months – but he promised that everything would soon be satisfactory. The Commissioners referred the case to H.M. Treasury, who decided that to give £20 was too much: even though the total cost of the alterations had now risen to £70, a grant of £18 was quite sufficient. Nevertheless, the school was 'reorganised and refitted' as the vicar had wanted. Probably it was at this time that the old paved floor (possibly from the 1822 building) was replaced by a wooden one, and two inside stone door frames were repositioned at the front of the building. Two dozen desks, each 7ft 6in. long were also installed in the two classrooms, with two dozen benches to match, which were screwed to the new wooden floor. After the alterations, the school remained closed until a new master and mistress were appointed. Later in the century the front of the building with the hat and bonnet closets was rebuilt, as was much if not all of the side and rear walls. In the east wall a window or doorway was filled in. Later still, extensions on three of the corners were added and the west wall window frames were replaced.

In 1870 Parliament passed the Elementary Education Act. Under it School Boards were appointed to set up elementary schools where they were needed, and one was set up to administer schools in the Forest. It was decided that, as the annual grant from the Office of Woods and other contributions were sufficient to run it, Parkend school should remain voluntary and not come under the control of the Board. However, the severe trade depression in 1879, which closed works and many collieries in Parkend, caused subscribers to cancel their contributions, and the school had to close as a result.

It re-opened on 1 June 1885 as a Board school. From now on we can consult the log books in which the head teacher or his deputy made entries most days and fascinating reading they make. Though the school was now under new management the buildings were still cold and draughty in winter – in January 1888 the children's hands were so cold that they were unable to write – and there was no artificial lighting until electricity was installed in 1937.

The head teacher had a hard job to ensure that all his charges attended regularly. The children often stayed away with their parents' connivance and sometimes the head had to turn them away because they had not paid their pennies, for state education was not free until 1891.

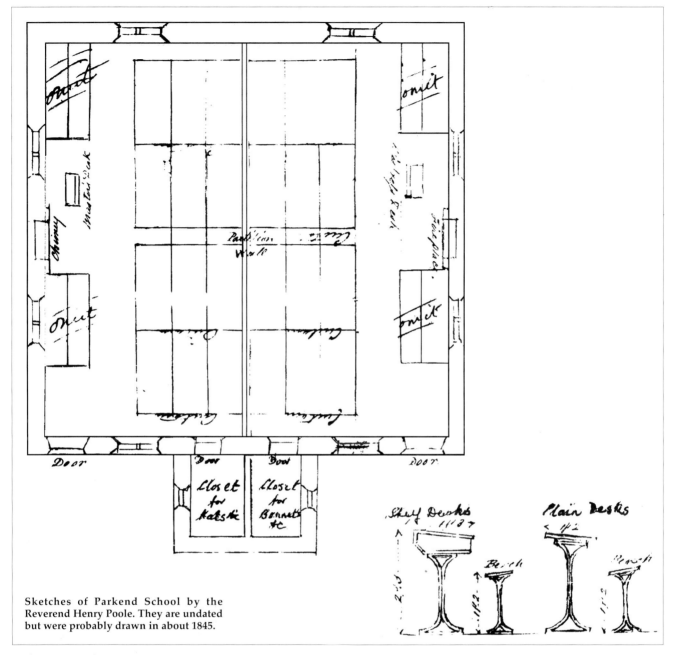

Sketches of Parkend School by the Reverend Henry Poole. They are undated but were probably drawn in about 1845.

There were other reasons for absences. In 1929 and twice in 1936 the children who lived in the Square (see page 40) were unable to leave their homes because they were flooded. In September 1893 many pupils absented themselves 'simply to see the horses being put down the pit again after the strike'; and on 13 February 1908 the children were taken down to the village for a most exciting happening, the felling of the ironworks chimney stack (see page 36).

The school was regularly closed for anything up to eight weeks because of infectious diseases – measles, scarlet fever, whooping cough, diphtheria or mumps. On several occasions it was closed because of a 'flu epidemic, the longest being in 1918 when the whole nation was engulfed and a million people died.

Royal occasions always provided opportunities to close. There was a week in 1897 to celebrate Queen Victoria's Jubilee, a week in 1902 for Edward VII's coronation and another week in 1911 for George V's. However, from then on closures for Royal occasions were restricted to one day.

Gradually, as the log books record, more and more was done to promote the health of the pupils. In 1885 boys were taken in military drill, and in 1911 there is the first record of a health lecture for the older girls. In 1916 a dentist's visit to the school is recorded, and in the same year there was a medical inspection. In 1928 hot cocoa was provided during the dinner hour; in the entries for 1933 there is reference to school milk and for 1942 to school dinners. Meals were provided at school for 'necessitous children' for about two months during the 1921 strike and for five months in 1926 during the lock-out in that year, during which the people of the Forest suffered unparalleled hardship.

The number of pupils attending the school has varied over the years. Nicholls said that it could hold 200, and in 1855, 158 pupils were attending. In 1865, however, the average number on the register was 85. In 1870 it had dropped to 58. The school re-opened in 1885 with about 70 children. In the

Parkend Council School groups. A note on the reverse of the top picture dates it as around 1913 and names the headmaster as Jesse Wintle. There is no information with the second view but the dress would suggest a late 1920s date, whilst on the right, a silver-haired Jesse Wintle was still the headmaster. The 1901 cenus shows Jesse Wintle to have been a native of West Dean, aged 27, and an elementary school teacher. He was the son of David Wintle of Yorkley a colliery engine driver.

1890s attendances averaged 125. In 1901 the figure was 112 and in 1905 it was 98. In 1997 was about 50 whilst in 2009 there are 55 on the register.

But back to 1857. In that year Henry Poole the vicar died after having served Parkend for nearly 40 years. He had devoted all his energies and his fortune to organising and helping to finance churches and schools in the Forest. In about 1830 he wrote:

> 'My troubles are chiefly of a pecuniary nature. Before I began the building of my parsonage my own means were nearly exhausted, having expended fully £1,000 of my own in the organisation of three churches, school houses and cottages to each ... Now in winding up my building debts I find I am fully £300 minus. This I am peremptorily required to pay without delay, which I am not able to do without the most formidable sacrifices and privations. I dare not apply to my own family for aid, for they are greatly displeased at my sinking my own property, not being able to enter into my motives for so doing'.

Henry Poole was buried, as was fitting, in the churchyard of Parkend Church under the East Window. One can just make out from the headstone that it was erected by his parishioners in grateful remembrance of his faithful services to their parish.

Baptist Chapel

There has been a Baptist Church at Parkend since 1862. It is one of the buildings in the row that faces the playing field, a dignified row of mostly l9th century buildings. While the Church of England church in the village was from the outset

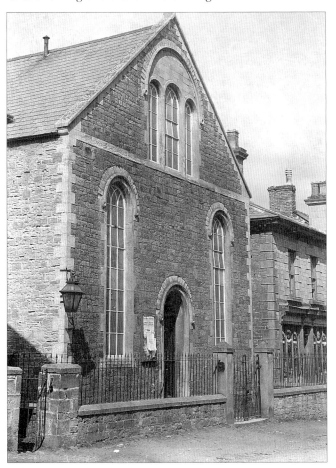

The Baptist Chapel, built in 1862. This photograph dates from around 1900.

intended to cover an area far exceeding that of Parkend, the Baptist Church was built for Parkend folk alone. The Coleford and Cinderford Baptist Churches played a large part in its planning and construction and one of its promotors was Alfred Pope, a tailor from Lydney. The land for the church was bought in April 1860 for £75, and the chapel was opened on 1 September 1862. The schoolrooms and baptistery followed in 1865. The total cost was £500. Of this, £200 was still owing in 1875, but it was paid off by 1883. The cost would have been more but the old Cinderford Baptist Chapel was being demolished at the time and its timber, slates, sills and windows were sold to Parkend for £100. The first pastor of the Church was William Nicholson, who had previously served the Lydbrook Church for 5 years. After Mr Nicholson there were often long periods during which the Church did not have its own pastor. However, for nearly 28 years, from 1891 to 1919, the Rev. S. J. Elsom filled the post. In the centenary year, 1962, the Church was redecorated inside and out, and made in a fit condition to weather the next 100 years.

The Kingdom Hall

The most recent religious building to be built in Parkend is the place of worship of the Jehovah's Witnesses. It is a fine stone building in traditional style, beautifully proportioned and stands a few yards up the Blakeney road from the *Woodman Inn*. It was built in 1991.

The Kingdom Hall, photographed in 1997.

Railway Cottages

The three houses west of Parkend Bridge, just opposite where the present *Fountain Inn* now stands, were probably built before 1700 (there may have been even earlier houses on the same site) and they must be three of the earliest dwellings in Parkend. The houses are now known as Railway Cottages and they have had a strange history. When steam trains came to Parkend in 1864, it was necessary to raise the road between these cottages and the *Fountain Inn,* on the other side, by about eight feet, to make a level run for the trains between the main railway line and the Marsh Wharf (see page 59). This meant that the ground floors of the houses on both sides of the road became cellars. Their first floors became level with the raised road and new front doors had to be inserted Another storey was then added, both to the Railway Cottages and the *Fountain Inn*. Also at this time, the *Fountain*'s striking semi-circular bay window was added. It replaced an earlier bay window, now in the cellar. Parkend Bridge would have been raised at the same time.

The *Railway Inn* on the Coleford to Blakeney road in the 1920s. The double track of railway is the line from Parkend Station to Cinderford, Lydbrook and Coleford. The single line, bottom right, serves the Parkend Royal Colliery. Top left is York Lodge.

Public Houses

There was probably a beer house of some sort in Parkend for as long as there had been a hamlet. In 1809 a contemporary wrote that there was 'no public house at Parkend', though he was probably thinking about an inn with accommodation rather than a place to have a drink, as he was complaining about not being able to find a bed for the night. The 1841 census records that there were two inns in the village in that year. As the number of inhabitants in Parkend at the time was only 78 (including children), the place was not very big and it is doubtful whether it could have supported two proper inns. During the 19th century there were, in addition to inn-keepers, 'beer retailers' who presumably ran what we now call off-licences or perhaps small drinking houses. There was also a beer house for a time at the ironworks.

By 1878 there were four inns or public houses in Parkend – the *Fountain Inn*, the *Traveller's Rest*, the *British Lion* and the *New Inn* (now *The Woodman*).

Reference has already been made to the *Fountain Inn* and how its ground floor became a cellar. The *Fountain*, which was in existence in 1841, closed in about 1976, but is now an inn again after being a guest house for a time. The *Travellers' Rest*, also called *The Bear*, was in existence before 1871. Later it was called the *Railway Inn*, although it was still known as *The Bear* when it closed in about 1959. It is now a private house. The *British Lion*, which opened in 1849, closed in the mid-twenties, and is now also a private house. Parkend also has a working men's club near where the *British Lion* used to be.

A view of *The Woodman* taken in 2009. Originally called *The New Inn*, the name was changed in the 1980s.

The *Fountain Inn* sometime in the 1930s. The railway connecting the Marsh Sidings to the main line runs immediately behind the fence on the left and crosses the road at the far end of the pub. The goods shed can be seen beyond that.

The *Fountain Inn* in about 1910. Margaret Gunter, wife of the landlord, stands by the front door.

A rare glimpse of Parkend Ironworks, probably taken a few years after ironmaking had ceased in 1877. In the centre can be seen the covered way which spanned the Severn & Wye Railway and allowed access to the tops of the furnaces for charging with coke, limestone and ore. On the left of the giant chimney, between it and the covered way, are the three furnaces, while on the right can be seen the engine house, the main surviving feature today. On the horizon, further right, is the tower of Parkend Church, nowadays concealed by trees.

Chapter 5
Industrialisation – the New Ironworks

Even though the King's ironworks in the Forest were closed in 1674 to help to conserve the forest trees for shipbuilding, other ironworks continued there. These other ironworks prospered for a time, but with the introduction of coke blast furnaces in the second half of the 18th century the old charcoal blast furnaces began to close down, until by 1816 they had all gone. The invention of the coke blast furnace resulted from improved technology which enabled coke to replace charcoal as the smelting agent for the iron ore. From now on the source of coal, not of charcoal or wood, was the prime factor in choosing a site for ironworks.

Parkend had plenty of coal, so was well placed to receive a new ironworks with a new coke blast furnace. One was set up there in 1799. Others were set up elsewhere in Dean at about the same time. The Parkend site was just north of the present railway station, a few hundred yards south of the old King's ironworks. The new works covered roughly the area now occupied by the village post office and store, but they were later to expand considerably.

The furnace was a single one and was powered by a steam engine. The blast was created by old-fashioned bellows at first, but they were soon replaced by blowing cylinders. By 1807 the works were being run by a Mr. Perkins, but it seems that the furnace was not capable of efficiently smelting Forest iron ore with coke made from Forest coal, and the works fell idle about this time. They were bought by John Protheroe, a local colliery owner, who early in 1824 sold them to his nephew Edward. Edward Protheroe, formerly a Member of Parliament for Bristol, was also a coalmaster, whose pits included some at Parkend. At this time Moses Teague, a metallurgist, was carrying out experiments in smelting iron with coke made from Low Delf coal at David Mushet's furnace at Darkhill. These experiments were no doubt aimed at solving the problems that had caused Mr. Perkins to close down. Edward Protheroe had plans for modernising the works, and in April 1824 was considering reopening them and operating them himself, perhaps with the knowledge derived from Teague's experiments. He decided, however, to lease them (on a 42 year lease along with some iron mines) to the newly-formed Forest of Dean Iron Company, which consisted of Teague, William Montague and Benjamin Whitehouse. They were later joined by John James of Lydney. In 1826 the partnership broke up and Montague and James became the lessees, with Teague as manager of the works.

The new Company were clearly at one with Protheroe in wanting to modernise and improve the efficiency of the works. By early 1827 they had erected a second furnace alongside the first. It was 45ft high, 9ft 6in. in diameter at the top, and 14ft wide at the base, like the first. They may also have rebuilt the first one at the same time; by now it was possibly in a poor state after having been disued for so long.

Also in 1827 the Company installed a waterwheel to supply power to create the blast for the furnaces. They clearly believed that even though steam engines had been in use for half a century – indeed Mr. Perkins had had one – they would be better off with water power. Sadly, the wheel was to prove an unprofitable investment, despite the trouble and expense to which the Company were prepared to go in an endeavour

to ensure a good and regular water supply for it by gravity from local streams. The new wheel, an over-shot, was 51ft in diameter, 6ft wide and 60 tons in weight. It was said at the time to be the largest in the Kingdom. The parts were cast in Gloucester and assembled in Parkend. It was most likely sited directly behind the present post office, where there was a recess about 50ft long and 7ft wide, bounded by the remains of a wall on one side and a building on the other. On the outer wall of the building were faint circular scratches which could have been caused by the wheel. [Building work in 2008 may have obscured this.] The building probably housed the cylinders which, worked by the wheel, provided the blast. The furnaces were in front of the building, on the site now occupied by the post office. The theory that the wheel was sited there is supported by the discovery of a clay water pipe running from there towards the Cannop Brook when sewers were being laid in the area in 1979. The pipe would have taken the water to the brook after it had moved the wheel.

The water for the wheel came mostly from a reservoir $1^1/2$ miles up the Cannop valley that the Company had created two years earlier by utilising the Severn & Wye tramroad embankment to dam the Cannop Brook at Bixslade to fill an old quarry, making what was to be known as the lower Cannop pond. Shortly after the brook had been dammed there were complaints of a reduction in the level of the water in the Lydney canal. Water was conducted from the lower Cannop pond along a man-made leat, over the Brookhall Ditches stream in a wooden aqueduct, and under the Blakeney road to a pond on the hill to the east of the ironworks. Most of the leat and the pond, now dry, can still be seen. From the pond the water flowed through a pipe to the wheel.

As the leat approached the pond, more water was fed into it from an auxiliary system built in 1826. This extra water came from the Drybrook and Oakwood brooks. A leat took some of the water from these brooks just below where they join one another (nearly a mile from the ironworks as the crow flies) and channelled it in a sweeping curve to the Coleford road a few hundred yards above the turnpike house, just below the Folly cottages. Here it went under the road and over the Darkhill stream through a pipe, part of which can still be seen. There is evidence that at some time the supply was augmented here by water from the Darkhill stream. The leat then continued, going under the Milkwall tramroad and along to a catch pool near York Lodge, sometimes called Parkend pool. The leat can still be traced along almost all its length. From the pool the water was channelled eastwards through a large iron pipe that went underground and surfaced again on the other side of the road and tramroad, and then joined the leat from the Cannop pond. The ironworks paid rent for this water up to about 1890.

A third source of water for the wheel was agreed at about the same time between the Iron Company and their neighbours, the owners of the Parkend stampers (see Chapter 6), under which the latter let the Iron Company have their water after it had turned their own smaller waterwheel. This water, it was said, came through some cast iron pipes laid in 1826 'at an expense of about £500'. These pipes were no doubt the ones linking Parkend pool to the Cannop leat.

The derelict but still majestic ironworks await their fate in this view taken about 1880. The three furnaces are to the left of the engine house; the two earlier ones are enclosed within the stone structure and the later steel encased furnace is on their right. In front of them are the casting sheds.

All the efforts to provide the ironworks wheel with a good supply of water were of little avail. In May 1827, only a few months after the first trial of the new wheel, the Company wrote to Edward Machen, the deputy Surveyor of the Office of Woods: 'We find, after the large sum we have expended and the precautions we have taken to procure water for the purpose of working our furnace here, that the supply is totally inadequate for the purpose. There remains therefore no other alternative but to erect a steam engine, this being the second time this twelvemonth in which our works have been stopped at a very great loss and expense and all the workmen discharged in consequence of the want of water to drive the machinery'. Machen could see no objection to the installation of a steam engine; but thought that the company 'should be obliged to build a stack of such a height that the smoke would be dissipated and rendered less injurious, which I believe on being called upon to do they would readily agree to'. Machen, who lived in nearby Whitemead Park, had good reason for

The lower Cannop Pond in the 1920s. Nowadays the preserve of fishermen and wildlife and a beauty spot for tourists, the pond was created in 1825 to feed water to the ironworks at Parkend, which lay a mile further down the valley.

insisting on a high stack!

The Company agreed and in about 1828 the engine (of 90 horse power) was installed in a new engine house, which still stands. However, even with this addition the power was inadequate, and in 1829, to boost the supply of water to the wheel, a second pond was constructed at Cannop. In 1834 there was a proposal to augment the supply yet again by taking still more water from the stampers' wheel after it had finished with it, but it is not known if anything came of the proposal.

No more is heard about the ironworks' wheel until 1841, when we learn that, for the one furnace that was working in that year, the blast was provided by the wheel in summer and the steam engine in winter, the reverse of what one would expect. In April 1842 James wrote to Machen complaining that the owners of the stampers were refusing to release sufficient water to him under the arrangement he had with them, and asking the Office of Woods to let his Company have the stampers' lease when it expired in a few months' time. This, he said, would ensure the ironworks their supply of water. He added that his Company were willing to take over the stamping mill as well. The Office of Woods were not disposed to fall in with James's suggestion but, when the stampers' lease was renewed, it stated clearly that the ironworks must have all the water they were entitled to. The licence under which James drew this water was renewed for 21 years in 1866.

In 1849 the existing supplies of power were again considered to be inadequate and another steam engine, this time of 80 horse power, was installed. In 1841 James had said that the wheel was being used 'only occasionally', so the installation of the new steam engine must have meant that it would now be used even less. Yet it does not seem to have been abandoned, because in 1866 there is a reference to water 'to be conveyed … to the Park End waterwheel'. But that is the last we hear of it. Despite all efforts to keep it moving, it seems never to have been a success. Indeed, considering the size and weight of this enormous structure, the layman may be forgiven for wondering how it ever moved at all!

Covered Ways
Another improvement that the Forest of Dean Iron Company carried out after leasing the ironworks concerned the bridge between the furnace and the hill on the east of it. From the evidence that has come to light, it seems that there were, at different times, three bridges.

At the end of the 18th century when the first furnace was built, it was customary to build furnaces close to or into a hill-side. Any gap between the hill and the top of the furnace was bridged, and over this bridge coke, iron ore and limestone were transported on the backs of horses and mules and tipped into the furnace-top. Part of the bridge was often covered over, usually the part over the furnace, and sometimes some of the bridge adjacent to it as well. The covered-in area was known as the bridge house. The whole was sometimes called the covered way. The first Parkend furnace was built near a hill, although the distance between it and the hill must have been about 20 to 30 yards, and it is difficult to understand why it was not built nearer. Perhaps it was initially nearer and the western side of the hill was later cut away to accommodate the tramroad (and later still the railway) that was to run between the furnace and the hill; but however near to one another they were initially, there must have been some sort of bridge between them. It was probably of a light structure, possibly of wood, since it did not have to bear very heavy weights. Access to the top of the hill and thence over the bridge to the furnace could have been up the long steady slope from the north, and one can visualise men and their pack-horses laden with iron ore, limestone and coal or coke slowly trudging across the sky-line.

Between 1810 and 1812 the Severn & Wye Railway Company built a tramroad from Lydney to Lydbrook through Parkend (see Chapter 7) and ran it between the ironworks and the hill. The first furnace had probably fallen into disuse by this time, and when the Company built the tramroad they would have adapted the bridge if it were in their way, or perhaps even have removed it altogether. So when first Edward Protheroe and then the Forest of Dean Iron Company arrived on the scene, the tramroad was there. In drawing up their plans for modernising the ironworks, they had to ensure adequate access to the top of the furnace and arrange for the water to run from the pond on the hill behind the ironworks to the waterwheel without losing any more height than was necessary. So they built a new bridge. It must have been an imposing structure, because it not only had tramroads and a large water pipe running across the top, but also had eight cottages incorporated in it. There also had to be, of course, a tunnel for the main tramroad that passed between the ironworks and the hill.

In June 1825 the ever watchful Edward Machen wrote to the Commissioners of Woods in London:

'The Forest of Dean Iron Company at Parkend have raised a very high mound of earth upon the Forest for the purpose of conveying the water to the top of the wheel they are proposing to erect and to bring the materials to the top of the furnace. To this I conceive no objection could be made, as it is a consequence of the permission to bring the water along the level laid down in the plan ... for a water course; but at the termination of this mound it becomes necessary to build walls to support the watercourse and wheeling way over an arch that is thrown across the railway. These walls the Company are now building, and observing that doorways and windows were left in them I addressed a letter to them saying that I did not consider they were authorised to make inhabited houses in this situation'.

Machen enclosed the Company's reply to his letter. It said:

'The walls we have built adjoining our premises at Park End over the Severn and Wye Railway were certainly in part intended to form buildings for the accommodation of our workmen without whose presence on the spot it would be impossible to conduct our works with much effect or profit. We beg to state that a part of the ground over which these tenements are intended to be erected is a portion of our own land which we gave up to the railway company for the purpose of making the road straight and that only two tenements would be required to be built over the land belonging to the Crown. We hope therefore that Hon. Commissioners will grant us permission to finish and occupy the two tenements in question, for the use of which we shall be glad to pay whatever acknowledgment the Commissioners may think proper to require'.

Unfortunately the records do not reveal the reply of the Commissioners, but there is no doubt that the bridge was finished with the eight tenements forming part of its walls, since it was recorded in 1841 that six out of the eight cottages 'under the bridge-house' were occupied. The size of the arched tunnel constructed round the tramroad was 10ft 4ins. high in the centre and, according to a Severn and Wye Company plan of 1856, most probably 14ft 2ins. wide.

In the 1850s and 1860s the Severn and Wye Company were considering laying a 7ft broad-gauge railway track next to the tramroad on which to run steam locomotives. It would have been difficult to do this in a tunnel 14ft 2ins. wide, and in 1859 the Company agreed to take down and rebuild the 'archway' as it was called, and improve the approaches to it. They did not apparently do this, since in 1866 they were considering the erection of a girder bridge about 90 yards north of the existing bridge. Then they seemed to revert to their earlier plan, and replaced the bridge on its old site, because in 1869 they told a Parliamentary Committee: 'We had a bridge at Parkend for some years, but the Iron Company wished to have a larger space on top, and joined the Company in the cost of building a larger bridge'. That the 1825 bridge was replaced by another is confirmed by an examination of the stone bases of the bridge, which still exist. They could not have been part of the bridge built in 1825, because they are 26ft 6ins apart, not 14ft 2ins. Further, an examination of the base on the furnace side shows clearly that it was grafted onto the part of the building against which the old waterwheel, installed in 1827, was positioned.

So a new bridge - the third - was built, with a wide enough tunnel to accommodate the 7ft railway track which was to be laid in 1868. The new bridge was built some feet north of the old one. It was wider at the top than the old one in order to give a better approach to the furnace tops (a third furnace was built alongside the other two in 1871). Measurement of the remains of the third bridge suggests that the new width was about 60ft It is likely that when the bridge was rebuilt the provision for the supply of water to the water-wheel was discontinued and that the wheel was abandoned at this time.

In addition to the furnaces and the bridge, surveys of 1835 and 1841 show that the works comprised a coke hearth, casting houses, engine houses, boilers, a carpenter's shed, a blacksmith's shed, a stable, a counting house and other workshops and offices, a beer house, a house for the agent, four good houses for workmen, and the famous eight cottages 'under the bridge-house'.

The iron ore for the furnaces came from the China Level and the China Engine mines in the Oakwood valley. Coal for the coke came from Fetterhill pit and the Parkend pits owned by Protheroe. In 1829 a large area on the hill opposite the ironworks was leased from the Office of Woods (for £5 a year) and made into what was called a coke yard. It was in fact an area where coke was made in the open and where materials to be put into the furnaces were assembled. The site had been purchased from the Office of Woods by 1878.

In July 1836 the Rev. Francis Witts from Upper Slaughter in the Cotswolds visited the Bathurst family who lived at Lydney Park. Among the trips they laid on for him during his stay was one to Parkend. He recorded details of his visit in his diary. They:

'took a delightful walk for two hours through the dense forest forming the background of the Park End forges and coalpits. Here we were at the centre of a busy, swarthy population, now in full employ, the coal and iron trade being very flourishing... The principal forge which we passed [is] in a gigantic grim mass of buildings, intersected by railway trucks [trams], abounding in steam engines, frowning like some timeworn fortress, whose huge dingy battlements resound with the clang of ponderous hammers, the blast of giant bellows, and similar impressive noises, now louder, now more suppressed as the varied operations proceed.'

In 1836 the Company leased from the Office of Woods an acre of land on which to deposit unwanted cinders from the furnaces. It was south of the works, east of the *Fountain Inn* and between the brook and the main tramroad. Machen insisted that the Company should erect a fence round the area 'of sufficient strength to keep the cinders within the boundaries of the acre allotted'. By 1848 the area was, in Machen's words, 'entirely covered and the cinders raised upon it to an inconvenient height'. James, one of the partners in the Company, had hoped that before the site overflowed the cinders would be wanted in connection with a steam railway it was proposed should go through Parkend, presumably for the track. As the railway had not materialised (indeed it did not appear for another 20 years) he asked the Office of Woods for another acre of land adjacent to the cinders mount on which he could dump more cinders. He proposed that the Cannop Brook should be diverted round the new area and, because the land was higher on the west, that a cutting seven to eight feet deep should be made there to take the diverted brook. His proposals were accepted by the Office of Woods and he was leased the land in 1850. In 1886 the lease was renewed. It was given up in 1901. Some 12,000 tons of cinders were removed and used as ballast between 1898 and 1904. The rest was used to make the New Road in 1903. As far as can be judged, the Cannop Brook has remained diverted.

Business in the iron trade was bad in Dean during the years 1829 to 1832, and there was seldom enough work for both furnaces during that time. In 1840 production of pig iron averaged only about 60 tons a week. In February 1841 it increased to 100 tons a week, but in the autumn the ironworks had ceased production 'because the iron trade in the Forest is in a greatly depressed condition'. In 1846, however, they reopened and prospered. In that year David Mushet junior praised the 'intelligence of the management' of the ironworks for their technical abilities; and in 1847 he wrote that 'the Parkend hot-blast iron possesses amazing strength. Mr. Montague, of Gloucester, the proprietor, has cast railway girders of most unusual power in proportion to their scantling: I have seen pigs of his iron deflect from 1 to 2 inches ere repeated blows could produce a fracture'.

In July 1847 James wrote to Machen seeking to lease land where the Parkend wharf was later to be built 'for the purpose of erecting [20] cottages and making gardens thereon for the use and convenience of workmen employed in the said iron and mine works, which are so necessarily connected, and the want of such cottages is at this time very severely felt by the workmen'. The reply was a refusal: the proposed cottages would be too near Mr. Machen's residence at Whitemead Park. James suggested an alternative site between the Brookhall Ditches tramroad and the Blakeney road. The site, he said, was 'wet in the winter', but 'capable of being drained, and is further from and more out of view from your House'. He promised that the proposed cottages would 'have a decent appearance such as need not be complained of'. This second proposal was also refused on the grounds that the legislation under which the Office of Woods could lease land did not cover this particular site. James eventually built his houses, now twelve in number, east of the ironworks at Mount Pleasant.

Montague died in 1847, and James obtained all his interests in the works and became sole lessee. In 1854 he bought the ironworks from Protheroe, from whom he had hitherto leased them, and from then on both furnaces were worked under the management of Charles Greenham, who had become a partner in the Company. The firm still continued to be known as the Forest of Dean Iron Company. James and Greenham now introduced iron forges and rolling mills into the works, and, as a separate venture, built a tinplate works nearby. By February 1864 the ironworks were producing about 280 tons of pig iron a week. At this time the works and the ore mining gave employment to about 300 men 'besides those engaged as colliers'.

In 1866 Greenham died, and James carried on alone. Business boomed and a third furnace was built in 1871. This was of a different design from the two earlier ones, being of the hot blast type. In this type, the blast of air blown into the furnace was heated, thus producing better quality iron. The two earlier furnaces had originally been cold blast, but they were later converted to hot blast. All three furnaces were in blast during most of 1871: the iron produced was used mainly for making Bessemer steel plates and tinplate. Then trade slackened and only two furnaces were required.

In 1875 a long slump descended on Dean. In that year Edwin Crawshay bought the ironworks and the tinplate works for £120,000, with the intention of establishing a limited company to operate them. The *Dean Forest Guardian* hoped and believed that with the new railway facilities now available there would be nothing to 'prevent the works being carried on with profit and great success'; but events did not support their optimism. We next hear that Henry Crawshay & Company were the owners. The Crawshay family owned other concerns in the Forest, and Henry, who died in 1879, was known as 'the Iron King of the Forest of Dean'. George Belcher of Parkend Cottage was now ironworks manager. The three furnaces were capable of producing 600 tons of pig iron a week, but such capacity was not required because of the depression. Production was further complicated by a fault at the China Engine mine which supplied much of the ore. Competition with ironworks outside the Forest that used cheap Spanish ore also contributed to the Crawshays' problems. From the end of 1876, only one of the furnaces was in blast, and in August of 1877 the works were closed.

This time there was no recovery, although the agony of dying was long. In February 1880 it was reported in the press that the works had been sold to the Ferro-Manganese Company Ltd who intended to make steel under the Ponsard Steel Patent; but this seems to have been a false report. In the summer and autumn of 1881 there were hopes of putting one of the furnaces in blast again, but they came to nothing. In January 1883 there were rumours that the works were to be sold and that new furnaces would be built at Whitecroft if negotiations for the sale collapsed. In May 1890 it was reported that the 'furnaces are being picked to pieces', even though one of them was working at a quarter capacity. But the end had come, and later in the year the furnaces were completely demolished. In 1892 the Crawshays were asked by the Office of Woods to renew the licence for the water from the Cannop ponds and the Oakwood, Darkhill and Drybrook valleys. They replied that the 'directors sometime since sold to Mr. T. H. Deakin the land, cottages and property that would benefit by the

A photograph of William Underwood (1833 - 1893), a Parkend ironworker with his daughters Sarah and Amelia. About 1872.

licences … and he wishes the same now transferred to him or his company (Deep Navigation Collieries Ltd.).' The lease was so transferred.

The covered way, by now in a dilapidated condition, was taken down in 1898, but the stone bases for it were left. There also remain: two dwellings known as Furnace Cottages; at right angles to them two single storey dwellings now used as out-houses; the building next to the site of the great waterwheel, now considerably repaired and used as out-houses; a foundry and moulding shop, which was sold by the Crawshays in 1896 to the Office of Woods for use as a carpenter's shop, afterwards used as a stable and now used by the nearby garage; a smaller building adjacent to the foundry originally a stable, then sold with the foundry to the Office of Woods as a store house for the carpenter's shop, and at present used by the garage; and, most important of all, the engine house that was built in about 1828 to provide power for the blast. This tall imposing building, which is next to the post office, became in 1910 after renovation the home of the first Forester Training School. During the Second World War 400 members of the Women's Land Army were trained there and the American Army also used the building for a time. The Forester Training School returned to it in 1946. In 1972 it became the Dean Field Study Centre run first by Avon County Council for teachers and secondary school children and now by Bristol City Council for primary and secondary school children.

The last ironworks' chimney stack was demolished in 1908. All that is left of the chimney is the rim from the top. It lies in the front garden of a farm near Bream, and serves as a container for garden plants.

FALLING CHIMNEY STACK AT PARKEND.

To prepare for the felling of the stack a hole a few brick courses in height was knocked out and pit props were jammed in position to hold the chimney, whilst the hole was widened to take in about half the circumference. Once the props were taking the weight of the stack, kindling and brushwood were placed around them and set alight. The fire burnt the props away and the chimney crashed down. The tiny figure leaning against the base of the chimney gives an indication of its size.

A dramatic photograph of the stack as it toppled. Note the spectators in the background.

The chimney is down. A picture taken after the dust had settled and much of the debris cleared away. Castlemain Colliery can now be seen on the hillside behind.

The conversion of the engine house was begun soon after the demolition of the chimney. Note the flimsy nature of the wooden scaffolding and the new windows already fitted. The builder responsible for the work was W. C. Nelmes of Berry Hill near Coleford; his name can be seen displayed on the scaffolding.

The Forester Training School at an interim stage of its development, around 1913, before the three-storey bay window and grand front entrance were added. An extension was also to be built on the side, probably added at the same time as the Post Office was built. The Institute had previously been located in a pavilion in the village and was to be forced out of this building by 1910 as the school expanded. The rear of Parkend Signal Box can be seen in the right background.

School of Forestry
Parkend.

The Class of 1928 Dean School of Forestry students and lecturers posed in front of the building.

Opposite: This study of the Forestry School, taken around 1930 by Cinderford-based photographer R. G. Gibbs, shows a low extension directly butted on to the end bay window added when the building was first converted which was soon all to be replaced by the work seen below.

A later 1930s photograph of the Forester Training School shows the alterations made to the engine house, including the three-storey bay and porch at the front, the extension to the far end and the new chimneys on the roof. Ivy now covers the original stone walls.

The Square, a group of dwellings built in 1851 for workers at the Parkend Tinplate works. In reality, the Square had only two sides, the two identical terraces of twelve houses each being built at right angles to each other. Some of the residents in this 1907 view have come out to pose for the photographer and note, too, the footbridge over the Parkend brook in the foreground.

The re-establishment of an ironworks at Parkend in 1799 was soon followed by the introduction of other industries into the village. In the early years of the 19th century a stamping mill was set up, and later came a tinplate works, a sawmills, lime kilns, a brick kiln and two stoneworks.

Stampers

Stampers were large machines that stamped or crushed slag from blast furnaces. Such machines had been in use in the Forest for many years before the advent of the coke blast furnace, but these older type stampers had been used to crush the iron ore itself (and perhaps bloomery cinders) to make it suitable for smelting in the charcoal blast furnaces. The stampers installed at Parkend at the beginning of the 19th century were for crushing into a fine powder the slag produced by the furnace after the extraction of the iron, so that it could be used to make glass, particularly bottle glass.

In the smelting process slag rose to the surface of the molten metal. This slag consisted mainly of a vitreous substance, but it also had some impurities and some granulated and scrap iron. The iron was separated in the stamping and reused. For glass making, bloomery cinders were apparently not suitable as they had too high a content of iron (40 per cent). The slag from charcoal and coke blast furnaces, however, with their lower iron content (30 per cent) was suitable. The former produced dark green glass, the latter light green to cream coloured glass.

In 1810 the Office of Woods licensed Isaac and Peter Kear to erect 'a stamping mill to reduce the powder, slag and cinders from the iron furnaces, for the use of the Bristol bottle-glass manufacture'. The Kears set up their mill west of the Blakeney road where it goes over the Cannop Brook, on the site of the old King's ironworks. In 1814 they were granted permission to use in their stamping mill the 'mound of cinders' on the land they had leased. These cinders had been there since the days of the King's ironworks and were estimated by David Mushet in about 1812 to weigh between 8,000 and 10,000 tons. The area came to be known as the stampers cinder mount. The Kears were also licensed to erect a waterwheel and were allowed to use water from the Cannop Brook to turn it. The water was not taken from the brook where it passed the stamping mill, as the mill was on higher ground, but from a weir about 1,100 yards higher up the brook. The water was conveyed along a leat that ran parallel with the brook to a small pond just above the waterwheel. At the same time, or shortly after, permission was granted to augment this water supply with water from the south. Only the last 200 yards of this course, called the stampers ditch, can now be identified. The leat and ditch may well have originally been water courses used by the King's ironworks (see page 13). The stampers site was clearly chosen because of the enormous load of cinders left by the King's ironworks, and possibly also chosen to take advantage of the water courses they also left behind.

In about 1823 James Ward and Thomas Holder joined the Kears in their ownership of the stampers. In 1828 Isaac Kear died, and his wife Mary inherited his share. Then Peter Kear died, and his widow married John Morse, who was now running the stampers. In about 1839 a new waterwheel costing £70 was erected, and in 1841 it is recorded that the proprietors were 'stamping ancient cinders with a 24ft waterwheel and 12 stampheads capable of returning 700 tons if there was a demand for it'.

In 1843 the stampers were owned by John Morse, Mary Kear, James Ward and Thomas Holder. The owners applied to the Office of Woods for a renewal of their licence. They said that 'the trade has been very much reduced over the last few years, and the cinders are a great distance from the stampers'. This presumably meant that they had used up the cinders left by the King's ironworks and now had to get their supplies from further afield. The licence was renewed from October 1843 for 31 years at £9 a year. In 1844 Mary Kear and Thomas Holder died. Mary Kear's interests passed to her two daughters, Betty Beach and Mary Hopkins, and Thomas Holder's to his wife Elizabeth. Mary Hopkins died in 1848, leaving her husband to look after her interest which had passed to her young daughter.

In December 1853 Morse wrote to the Commissioners of Woods in London that there had been no work for the stampers for two or three years. 'There has been no demand for the scruff for the last five years in consequence of another company at Redbrook working against us at a lower price than we can render it. Therefore the works by lying idle are so much out of repair that a considerable sum must be laid out in repairs to put them in working condition'. He asked for the rent due the previous Michaelmas to be cancelled so that he could repair the works by the following spring. Machen, from Whitemead Park, confirmed that no work had been done by the stampers for several years 'and in consequence there has been no diminution in the quantity of cinders in the Forest'. The reply from London was that the rent must be paid, but the licence could be cancelled if this were desired.

It is not known whether the rent was paid, but in 1855 James Ward wrote asking for the licence to be cancelled. He said that the works had been shut for some time and were not likely to be opened again, and that Morse had bought out the other partners. Morse, however, asked for the licence to be issued to him alone, and after eight leisurely years of consultation with various parties, the Office of Woods granted him the licence for 31 years, again at £9 a year.

In 1859 Morse bought from the Office of Woods some land to the west of the stampers cinder mount, and built a house on it in which he lived. Appropriately enough, he called it 'Stampers Cottage'. It is still there. In 1865 the Office of Woods gave him permission to erect a stable on the cinder mount. In 1893 the lease for the stampers ground expired, and Morse applied for its renewal for ten years. The deputy Surveyor of the Office of Woods reported that 'very little work has been done by the stampers in the last ten years, so I am informed, and certainly no work has been done for some time, for the stampers and waterwheel are in a ruinous condition'. Under earlier leases Morse had leased water from the Darkhill and Drybrook valleys which, as the deputy Surveyor said, had once flowed 'along a course at the back of certain houses… no water flows along the course now,

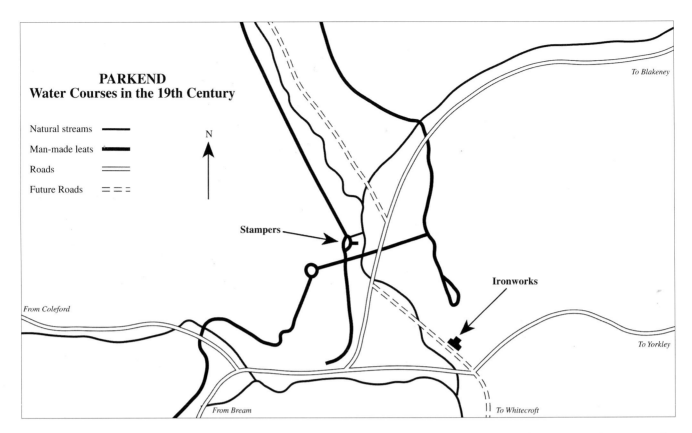

PARKEND
Water Courses in the 19th Century

Natural streams ───
Man-made leats ▬▬▬
Roads ═══
Future Roads ═ ═ ═

N

Stampers

Ironworks

To Blakeney

From Coleford

To Yorkley

From Bream

To Whitecroft

---

nor has it flowed for some years, and the course has become a series of stagnant cess pools at the backs of these houses, causing a great nuisance and highly injurious to health.' Because the stampers had an ample water supply from the Cannop Brook, the Office of Woods decided to exclude from any renewed lease the land along which this ditch ran (the ditch, however, remained outside the back doors of the houses until it was paved over in the 1920s).

In the end Morse did not take up the new lease. Instead he settled for leasing the land on which he had built the stable. He died at a ripe old age in 1911. Until recently the eight cottages behind which the stagnant ditch ran were called Stampers Row. Alas, that little reminder of what had once been at the end of the lane is fading. The cottages are now officially known as Hughes Terrace, after the Hughes family, one of whom, James Hughes who owned a wood sawmill in the village, built the cottages in 1859. All that is left of the activities of the stampers are lumps of slag, on or just below the surface of the land on which they stood.

Tinplate

The tinplate works adjoined the ironworks on the north, and lay to the east of the present playing field between the Cannop Brook and the tramroad. They included iron forges and rolling mills, and were built in 1851-53 by John James and Charles Greenham, who already leased the Parkend ironworks. Tinplate is steel (originally sheet iron) that is given a thin coating of tin. Tinplate works began to appear in the Forest in the second half of the 18th century. At first they used charcoal as fuel, later coke. Making tinplate in the l9th century was an unpleasant and dangerous occupation. It involved dipping iron sheeting into boiling grease and pickling it in sulphuric acid, which sometimes affected the eyes and stomachs of the men and women involved. The plate was cut by powerful machine-driven shears and the fingers of the operatives were frequently cut off accidentally. Cases are also recorded of people at the Parkend tinworks having fingers crushed in the sheet rolling mills and scalding themselves in boiling grease.

The setting up of the tinplate works did not meet with the approval of Mr. Machen, the deputy Surveyor. He wrote a letter from Whitemead Park to the Commissioners in London in February 1851, in which he said that he was not in a position to comment on the tinplate works as they were being built on James and Greenham's own land. However, he thought it right to say that 'I expect that these tinworks will be a considerable drawback in the comfort of this house as a residence, the increase of smoke and the noise of forges (for I conclude they are to include forges) will be less than the offensive smell, as they use quantities of vitriol and grease in the tinworks. The distance is about 400 yards. I don't know any means of stopping it'.

Once the construction of the tinplate works was under way James and Greenham took out a 31 year lease on some Crown land just north of the works and built twenty-four houses on it for their workers. The houses were three storeys high and had six rooms each and, because they were laid out in two blocks of twelve roughly at right angles to each other, they came to be known as the Square. During the 20th century they were owned by William Hughes, the proprietor of the Parkend sawmills. They were demolished in the mid-1950s, and their inhabitants were rehoused in the Council estate on the outskirts of the village. One reason for this demolition was the flooding that in later years they frequently underwent in winter from the overflowing of the Cannop Brook which passed nearby. The reason the brook became swollen so regularly has been ascribed to water from closed pits which, instead of being pumped away in other directions, found its way into the Cannop Brook. Latterly the houses of the Square were not kept in a good state of repair by the owner, and a contributory reason for their demolition was probably their insanitary condition. They had no indoor lavatories or septic tanks, only buckets whose contents had to be disposed of as well as possible. One must remember that there was no main drainage in Parkend until 1979, although most of the houses had perfectly hygienic drainage systems before then.

In March 1853 James asked the Office of Woods to lease to his Company an acre of ground near the Brookhall Ditches stream on which he could deposit rubbish and cinders from the tinplate works. The ground was near the tramroad in a hollow and was probably an old stone quarry. The Office of Woods agreed but Machen, cautious as ever, required James to acknowledge that it was 'for this purpose only'.

James and Greenham did not keep the tinplate works long after they had built them. By the autumn of 1854 they were owned by Samuel Ries. Ries leased them to Nathaniel Daniels who traded as the Parkend Plate Company. Daniels was not very successful. He was insolvent by December 1854, and a Trustee was appointed to sell the assets. In 1856 the works were bought by Thomas and William Allaway who had been running tinplate works successfully at Lydbrook and Lydney. They enlarged and improved the works and, as the Rev. Henry Poole the local vicar reported, carried them on 'with much spirit and success'. By 1866 they were employing 200 workpeople and producing about 500 boxes of tin plates a week. Two-thirds of the iron they used was made in the Forest.

In 1872 the works were put up for auction. The notice advertising the sale stated that they comprised about seven acres of freehold land, the fixed plant, machinery and rolling stock; also included were an excellent house suitable for the proprietor, a manager's house (probably Brook House), storehouses, warehouses, offices, carpenter's and blacksmith's shops, stables and the twenty-four houses known as the Square 'all in excellent tenentable repair'.

In 1875 Edwin Crawshay bought the works, and in the following year it was producing 700 to 800 boxes of tinplate a week. However, the slump of 1875 to 1878 had arrived, and

Crawshay's prosperity was short-lived. The fortunes of the works were no doubt bound up with those of the ironworks which he also owned. In January 1877 both works were taken over by Henry Crawshay & Son, and in August of that year both ceased production. By 1878, according to the Ordnance Survey map of that year, the tinplate works were 'disused', but the next year they were let to Charles Morris of Llanelly on a 14 year lease. Gangs of workmen began to clean up the premises and renovate the machinery. The *Dean Forest Guardian* promised that shortly 'the inhabitants of this village may expect to see and hear the familiar sights and sounds so gratifying to them, but which for so long a period have been withheld'. In 1880 both mills were working, and the 1881 census showed that in that year more people in Parkend worked for the tinplate works than for any other industry.

However, the revival was short-lived. In August 1881 Morris gave a month's notice to his workers terminating their monthly contracts, and offering to replace them by day-to-day contracts. The *Dean Forest Mercury* wondered what his real intentions were in issuing the notices. 'The mills are now in first class working trim, and it can hardly be supposed there is any intention of stoppage; such an event will be deplored and it is hoped that the lesser evil only is intended, viz, some adjustment of the wage rate'. The tinplate workers accepted the revised terms, but Morris nevertheless closed the works. Two hundred employees were paid off on 21 September - eleven days after they had accepted the revised terms of employment. The *Mercury* hoped that 'the shadow again cast upon Parkend may be speedily removed'; but it was not. In May 1882 Jacob Chivers and Company, who had considered buying the works from the Crawshays in 1878, reconsidered the matter but finally decided not to buy them. The works did not open again. For a time they stood derelict. In the early 1900s they were demolished, and nothing now remains. It has been said that the cause of the failure of the works was threefold: the unsuitability of the local iron ore for the Bessemer process of converting specular cast iron into the type of steel most suitable for tinplate; competition from South Wales; and a falling market generally.

The dilapidated rear of the Square. This picture was taken shortly before the dwellings were demolished in the 1950s.

The main entrance to the sawmills in the 1920s.

Sawmills

There have been sawmills in Dean for hundreds of years. By 1614 there were at least eleven sawpits in operation, and others were set up later. In the 19th century larger and more efficient sawmills were introduced. James Hughes, who was born in 1829, the son of a woodman from Parkhill, had a sawmill in Parkend from at least 1859. His premises were between the Baptist Chapel and the *New Inn* (now *The Woodman*), behind the house now known as the 'Mill House'. Power for the mill was supplied by a waterwheel, the water for which probably came from the stampers ditch which ran past the mill to the stampers wheel. In 1900 Hughes took a lease on York Lodge as a residence, but he also used some of the outhouses as storage places for his wood business. Included in the lease was 'the meadow in front of the post office'. The post office in those days was next to the Baptist Chapel, and the meadow is now part of the village playing field. In 1901 James Hughes died and his son William continued with the business. During the Hughes ownership it was called the Steam Saw Mills as a steam engine was used, presumably to supplement or replace the waterwheel. The water for the engine was pumped from the Oakwood brook nearby.

The business seems next to have been owned, in part at least, by the Office of Woods, although it was still called Hughes' Sawmills. In 1918 the Office of Woods' carpenter's shop near the present garage was transformed into a stable to house ten horses for the sawmills, and the carpenter's shop was transferred to Hughes' old timber storing shed. Then Bartlett, Bayliss and

On 26 May 1928 the sawmills were burnt to the ground.

Company Ltd bought the business and moved it about 50 yards to the west. The sawmills were burnt to the ground on 26 May 1928. No-one was badly hurt, and the mills were later rebuilt. In 1932 or 1933 the business was bought by William Rivers who in 1933 formed Parkend Sawmills Ltd. He was succeeded by his son Leslie Rivers. At this time and probably for some time before, a wheelwright carried out his trade on the premises. There was also a blacksmith who shrank iron rims onto the wheels made by the wheelwright. Horses were shod there until 1950. The business ceased trading about 1972, and the buildings fell into disrepair. In 1975 James Joiner bought the site and enlarged it, taking in part of the track of the railway that had run to Coleford until the line was closed in 1967. In 1977 it was sold to International Timber, who introduced modern equipment and replaced the old buildings with modern ones. International Timber, however, is not a sawmill for local wood; it is a depot where imported hardwood is kilned and stored.

Inside the Parkend Sawmills, showing one of the heavy duty saws being used to cut a Forest tree trunk into planks. This was often arduous and noisy work, and a number of sawmill workers lost fingers, hands and, on rare occasions, part of an arm to the unprotected saw blades.

A Unipower Forester tractor belonging to Parkend Sawmills, hauling newly felled logs out of the Forest shortly after the Second World War. The tractor possibly arrived at Parkend from America under the lend-lease arrangements during the war.

Brick Making and Blacksmiths' Shops

There was a brick kiln on the left of a path that ran eastwards past a blacksmith's shop near Parkend Wharf to the tinplate works. The brickyard was in existence in 1840 when it was run by Christopher Morris. It was still there in 1880, but had gone by 1900, as had the blacksmith's. There was also a blacksmith's at the wood sawmills in the early years of the 20th century, if not before.

Lime Burning

Limestone has been quarried and burnt to produce lime in the Forest from Roman times and perhaps earlier. The lime was used as a manure and for making mortar. In 1787 there were 21 lime kilns in the Forest. In Parkend in the 19th century there were three lime kilns on Mount Pleasant.

Stone Quarrying & Working

Stone has been quarried and worked in Dean since at least 1800 BC. In 1841 there were 320 quarries active, and 10,000 tons of worked stone were being turned out. The first reference to stone works in Parkend concerns the stone sawing machinery installed at the Parkend Stone Works by Hall and Hall, a London firm, in 1850. These works were west of the Blakeney road, just past the railway crossing. In 1889 they were owned, together with 15 quarries, by David and Company. At that time the machinery comprised 6 horizontal sand and water saw frames, 3 planing and moulding machines, one circular rubbing table, several lathes, and an overhead gantry. Sixty masons were employed and the machinery was kept working night and day. After an amalgamation in 1892, the company was known as David and Sant Ltd, and by 1899 the number of quarries owned had risen to 41. Between 300 and 350 men were employed by the company at Parkend and in the quarries. Day-work wages were about 4/4d (22p) a day; contract work was better paid. Some stone came from the company's quarries at Bixslade, other stone from Portland in Dorset. A railway siding connected the works with the main line to Lydney.

In 1900 the company was acquired by the Forest of Dean Stone Firms Ltd. who in turn were taken over in 1910 by United Stone Firms Ltd. They were soon in difficulties and in 1913 they went into receivership but continued trading under the receiver until in 1926 Walter Bryant formed United Stone Firms (1926) Ltd. Some of the stone for the BBC building in Portland Place, London, built in the 1920s, was dressed at the Parkend Stone Works. The works closed in 1932 following the liquidation of United Stone Firms (1926) Ltd. On the site there are still two enormous stones which can be seen from the road. Originally they were destined for the front entrance of Harrods Store in London but they proved too hard to dress. As a result they stayed in their rough state in Parkend and constitute all that is left of the works. The site is now occupied by the Forest of Dean Caravan Company.

Also at Parkend were stone works belonging to E. R. Payne and Son Ltd. These works were established by 1870. Their site was just south of the Parkend Stone Works, on the other side of the railway line, behind the *Railway Inn*. The stone came from the company's quarries at Bixslade and Barnhill. The Company also owned Point Quarry, which is on the right of the road leading to Coleford, about a mile out of Parkend above the old railway line. This, and other quarries adjacent to it, are well worth visiting.

In 1910 the company was also taken over by the United Stone Firms Company Ltd. who, as seen above, were soon in trouble. According to the liquidators who were called in, United Stone Firms had never taken the trouble to find out exactly what they had taken over from Payne's, and they had continued, among other things, to pay rent for quarries that were exhausted. It seems that Payne's Parkend works closed in 1910 or 1911 as the siding into it was removed in 1911.

The Forest of Dean Stone Firms' works were situated alongside the main railway line between Travellers Rest Crossing and Coleford Junction. Some wagons can be seen at the junction, beneath the overhead gantry crane. The stoneworks also had their own steam-driven rail-mounted crane, seen here on the left. The blocks of stone were moved around the site via rail-mounted trolleys, one of which appears in the right foreground. The site is now occupied by Forest of Dean Caravans. Photograph taken in about 1910.

The Forest of Dean Stone Firms' works seen from The Tumps, where the council estate now stands, in about 1925. In the background is York Lodge. The houses that nowadays surround the junction of the Lydbrook road with the road to Blakeney have not yet been built.

A group of stoneworkers at the Parkend works, around 1910. The stone blocks weighed several hundredweight each. The man standing in the right foreground holding a pick is the foreman, William Dobbs.

Parkend Station around 1900. The remains of the ironworks dominate the background and York Lodge can be seen on the hillside in the left distance.

Chapter 7
Roads, Tramroads and Railways

Roads and railways came late to Parkend. There were no roads through the centre of the Forest in Roman times, probably because the Romans had no need for them: iron ore was not found in the central part of the woods, only on its fringes. Even if the Romans had wanted roads they would have had difficulty in making them, because there was marshy ground at Ruspidge on the east, at Mierystock at the northern end of the Cannop Valley, and at Parkend at the southern end. The road nearest to Parkend in Roman times ran from Highfield just east of Lydney to Soudley, and then on to Littledean, Abenhall, Mitcheldean and the Roman settlement of Ariconium. Part of this road can still be seen at Blackpool Bridge.

After the Romans left, their roads decayed. All the Forest had then, for over a thousand years, were tracks. Camden, writing towards the end of the 16th century, refers to crooked winding paths and crossways, which penetrated the Forest depths and which twisted and turned to avoid streams, bogs and thickets. These paths were not possible for wheeled vehicles. However, north of the central part, from Mitcheldean to Monmouth there was a road at least from Elizabethan times.

The first mention of any money being spent by the Crown on making or improving roads in the Forest is in about 1760, when plans were made for a road from Mitcheldean to Coleford, and one from Littledean to Coleford. These two became the principal roads for the traveller going from Gloucester to South Wales. Apart from these, there were at the time no other roads worthy of the name in the Forest.

Wagons, especially coal wagons (for by now coal mining was a growing industry) used what tracks there were, but these were poor and impassable in winter, and were abandoned when the tramroads arrived. At this time timber for the Navy was taken from the Forest via Blakeney.

A map dated 1777 shows that at that time the only roads out of Parkend were one to Yorkley and one to Coleford, with a branch to Clearwell Meend. In 1795 more money was spent on Forest roads, including the Coleford to Yorkley road, which now went on to Viney Hill. In 1823 there was still no road, or even a path, going from Parkend up the Cannop valley, but there was a path direct to Speech House. There were paths to Bream and Whitecroft, but no roads.

The Government does not seem to have spent any more money on roads in the Forest until 1828, when they financed the construction of several roads, including one from Parkend to Bream. This was a toll road, and the toll house is still in existence a quarter of a mile up the Coleford road where the road to Bream branches off. Originally it was a single storey building, but in 1906 it acquired a first storey. The toll had an agent appointed to collect the tolls on behalf of the Commissioners, and in 1856 the agent collected £143 5s. 2$\frac{1}{2}$d. In 1841 the Parkend to Blakeney road via Moseley Green was built. This was also a toll road. Turnpikes on roads were abolished in 1888, when the full financial responsibility for maintaining roads was taken over by the central government and county councils. In 1903 the road down the Cannop valley through Parkend and on to Whitecroft and Lydney came at last, and the present network of main roads was established.

This photograph of the road out of Parkend at the Travellers Rest Crossing is one of the earliest views known of a Forest of Dean location. It dates from around 1870. The road was constructed as a turnpike in 1841 and this view, about thirty years later, shows the state into which it had lapsed. The Severn & Wye main railway line runs across the picture, with the narrower gauge tramroad just in front of it.

The Parkend Turnpike on 31 October 1888, the day before the Dean Forest Turnpike Trust was abolished and the roads were made free. Crossing the road in front of the house is the Oakwood tramroad.

Station Cross in the 1920s, looking up the road towards Yorkley and Viney Hill. The shop and cottage on the left were demolished in the 1960s and the signal box disappeared with the closure of the railway north of Parkend in 1967. The road through Viney Hill led eventually to Purton, on the banks of the Severn, and was the main route out of the Forest for naval timber in the late 18th century.

A general view of the village in the 1920s, with the Square prominent in the centre and the colliery chimneys smoking away in the background. In the centre distance can just be seen the Council school. Mr Morton, the photographer, moved to Parkend in around 1920 and lived here for about 10 years. Little is known about him, except that he originally came from Hereford, where he also published local postcard views, and also that for a while he rode around on a Wattney motorcyle, manufactured by Watts of Lydney.

New Road, built around 1903, looking towards the Forestry school and the church. The road ran across land formerly occupied by both the ironworks and the tinplate works. The cottage up on the left is Mr. Rees's house (see page 59). The picture dates from the 1920s.

Another view along New Road, showing on the left the '1910 house' as locals know it, so-called because that was the year it was built for the manager of New Fancy Colliery. The semi-detached houses next door were built in the following year. The playing field lies behind the row of poplar trees to the right, which were felled in the 1960s. They were the only Lombardy poplars in the Forest.

The Post Office and general store, run by R. Thomas, in a view taken by Morton around 1925. This row of buildings was most probably erected around 1912. Happily, the post office is still open and has not been a victim of the savage cull of more rural offices. It is not possible to positively identify the delivery van in the background but Downham Bros bakery at Bream had a similar vehicle which delivered to Parkend.

New Road, Parkend

Two views along New Road in the early to mid 1950s, possibly taken by the Cinderford photographer Chapman. In the view above looking towards the railway station, a solitary motor car is parked outside the Post Office and may well have been the photographer's own vehicle. It was most probably taken on the same day as the view below as the car is in the same position albeit the blind at the Post Office has been put away. The end of the Forester Training School has been altered with the addition of a fire escape, prior to this ropes from the windows were used. The building on the left was demolished in the 1970s.

New Road, Parkend

Fancy Road, the Coleford to Blakeney road, in the early 1950s. Next to the grocer's shop on the left (now long closed) are, first a private house, then the Memorial Hall and beyond that the Post Office. The Baptist Chapel next door is set back but its roof can be seen above the former Post Office. In the centre distance, where the road starts to climb, is Travellers Rest Crossing, whilst on the right is the playing field with one of the terraces of The Square visible beyond. On the extreme left are the back doors of Kear's bakery delivery van, Kear's were based at Whitecroft.

The road to Coleford and Bream from Parkend in the mid 1930s. The Pike House can be seen in the distance. The fence on the left marks the boundary of Whitemead Park. The Oakwood tramroad ran along the verge on the right.

These two postcard views of the *Fountain Inn* and level crossing were taken from similar positions but approximately thirty-five years apart. The *Fountain* has changed from being the *Fountain Hotel* to the *Fountain Inn* whilst in the upper view the now demolished Parkend House can be seen amongst the trees which in the intervening years have grown to hide it in the lower scene. That apart, and the 1960s road vehicles, the slightly improved road surface and the arrival of a red telephone box, there had been few changes over the years. Note the weeds growing in the track of the Parkend Marsh Branch in the lower view, although it was still in regular use at this time.

New Road in the mid 1960s, showing little change from a couple of decades earlier apart from the road vehicles. This postcard is in the same series as the one of the *Fountain Inn* on the previous page.

This sylvan view of a woodland path, with bridge across the stream, is believed to be off New Road, just to the south of the village and on the footpath between Whitemead Park and Parkend Church. The distinctive handwriting of the caption marks out the photograph as the work of Gibbs of Cinderford. Postcard collectors should be able to use this knowledge to identify several other pictures in this book as his; Gibbs in fact covered most areas of the Forest of Dean but never signed his work.

A bogie tramroad wagon on the Bixslade tramroad. Such wagons and loads would have been a common site around Parkend.

Tramroads

The lack of reasonable roads to serve Parkend until well into the l9th century must have delayed the full industrialisation of the village. Even before the l9th century dawned, industrialisation was restive to expand in the Forest and, with the introduction of the coke blast furnace, more intensive working of the iron and coal mines by bigger men than free miners was waiting to start. Transporting raw materials by pack mules or horse and cart over the primitive roads was not enough, and pressure for a tramroad network from local and neighbouring industrialists mounted. So the tramroads came to the Forest.

It may be helpful to explain what a tramroad was. Railway lines are flat on the top and the trains are prevented from falling off by flanges on the wheels. In tramroads the opposite was the case: the tracks were flanged plates, like an L, and the tram wheels were flat. In the early 19th century these tramroads were usually called railroads or railways. Later they were called tramways. In fact a tramway was a later development than the tramroad and was really a narrow gauge railway worked by horse, rope or locomotive power. Another name for a tramway was a plate way; and in the latter half of the l9th century tramways were sometimes called trolley roads. To simplify matters we shall call them all tramroads.

The rails, or plates, of the tramroad were made of cast iron and were 3ft long at first; later they were made of wrought iron and became 6ft and then 9ft long. The rails were laid on stone blocks at least 14ins. square and 7ins. thick. The end of each rail notched on to the end of the next one and formed a square hole through which a 5 inch nail was driven into an oak plug that had been placed in a hole in the stone block. When it was found that the nail was not securing the rails properly, a chair or saddle was placed between the rail and the stone. The rail was held in the chair by a wooden wedge or wedges, and the chair was secured by two nails fastened into the stone by molten lead. Most of the blocks you can

still find in the Forest have three holes. (The blocks on the Birches branch near Parkend have only one.) The gauge was originally 3ft 6ins; later the stones on which the plates were laid spread apart and the gauge became more like 3ft 8ins. The wagons varied in size, but by 1843 they all had to have four wheels at least 1ft 9ins. in diameter and at least $^7/_8$ in. wide at the rim, They were pulled by horses, ponies or mules, which were not allowed to go faster than at a walk.

Tramroads were quickly and cheaply built. They followed the contours of the land and few bridges or tunnels were necessary. As maps of the same area at different times show, their position was often changed, probably without too much difficulty.

The great difference between the tramroads and the railways was that the tramroads were used like a public highway. They were in effect toll roads. The owners of the merchandise to be moved had to provide trucks and arrange with hauliers for horses and drivers to move them. The owners of the tramroads provided little but the track and weigh-houses where the rates to be charged were assessed. The railways, on the other hand, when they arrived, provided engines, stations, goods yards and signalling systems; so their tracks were in no way comparable to a public highway.

Tramroads, like many other things, came to Dean later than to other parts of Britain. The first tramroad in the Forest was built in 1795 by a free miner, James Teague, from his Engine Pit at Perch Hill, near Edge End, to a road nearby. In the following year he built another, longer one from the pit to the River Wye. He did not apply to the Forest authorities for permission to build the part of the track that ran through the Forest and the acrimony between them and Teague, which lasted twenty years, resulted in unsuccessful legal action being taken by the Attorney General in the Exchequer Court. In 1815 James Teague abandoned the tramroad when he had no further need for it.

By this time an extensive system of public tramroads had been set up in the Forest. The Bullo Pill Railway Co.

(renamed the Forest of Dean Railway Co. in 1826) operated tramroads in the eastern part of the Forest; the Monmouth Railway Co. operated in the west, linking the Forest with Coleford and Monmouth; and the Severn & Wye Railway & Canal Co. operated in the centre and linked the two rivers. The Severn & Wye were the biggest company and Parkend came into its area. When the Company surveyed Parkend in 1809 to determine the best route for the tramroad, they considered taking it between the Cannop Brook and the furnace; but, in the event, they laid it on the other side of the furnace between it and the hill on the east. By 1811 they had practically completed the whole length from Lydbrook on the Wye to Lydney on the Severn, with branches to serve local mines, quarries, furnaces, forges and tinplate and wire works. Thus they enabled industrialists to transfer their merchandise to other places on the tramroad system and to navigable waters.

Parkend was a focal point in the network: the main line went through it; four branches, the Ivy Moor Head, the Brookhall Ditches, the Milkwall and the Oakwood branches converged here; and the Birches branch joined the main line a little to the south of the village. The Ivy Moor Head branch was built in 1809 or 1810 to serve the pit there, and in 1827 Edward Protheroe extended it to his Parkend Royal and Land Royal pits. By 1835 there were sidings to Parkend Main, Catch Can, Standfast and Staple pits, and also to the Parkend ironworks. In 1813 a branch was made along the Brookhall Ditches stream to serve the Brookhall Ditches pits owned by Protheroe. Later, when leased to the Parkend Coal Company, they ceased production and the line was taken up by the company's manager 'because they would never want to use it again'. In 1824, owing to stoppage at its Birches pit, the company found that they did indeed want to use it again, and asked the Severn and Wye company to replace the rails. The Severn and Wye did so, but made the coal company pay for the reinstatement and reimbursed them from tolls as they became due.

A branch to the Milkwall area was built in 1812 to bring iron ore from there to Parkend. It also served pits and quarries at Darkhill and other places on the way. By the middle of the 19th century the stretch from Fetterhill to Parkend was a very busy area, with stone quarries on both sides of the valley, stone mills, houses and a public house. Now only a few houses, some ruins and a quarry or two remain. From the centre of Parkend, the Milkwall line ran parallel to the road that goes past the *Fountain Inn*. Then it turned north-west along a wide track still known locally as 'the tramroad'. From here the track crossed the Coleford road and then ran parallel to it. Later a branch was built off to the left to serve the Venus colliery. The tramroad originally looped round the back of a small group of cottages called Western Cottages. Later it was re-routed cutting out the loop, and later still, when the railway arrived, it was re-routed again, this time south of the railway line. The tramroad then ran along the hillside past some stone quarries, across the Coleford road and on to Milkwall. Later, when the railway arrived, it was re-routed under the railway line through a tunnel, which is still extant, to serve Point and David quarries. In 1819 an extension to the tramroad was made a little further up the track to serve David Mushet's newly-built ironworks at Darkhill.

It was here that Mushet carried out some of his experiments to improve the making of iron and steel. The ruins of these works were tidied up in the late 1970s and the walls partly reconstructed, as part of a Manpower Services Commission scheme. The sight of them as one comes along the railway track that flanks them is quite breathtaking. The large lake nearby is filled with red-brown water, still giving a clue to its former association with iron.

Nearby is what is left of the Titanic Steel Works, built about 1863 by David Mushet's son, Robert Forester Mushet. Here Robert made the world's first self-hardening tool steel that he had perfected. This steel was a great success but the works were closed in 1871 and production transferred to Sheffield. All the buildings that originally made up the works have disappeared except one which, in spite of its slightly lozenge shape and shortage of windows, is now used as a private house.

In about 1826 David Mushet built the Oakwood tramroad. It branched off the Milkwall tramroad just after the latter had left the centre of Parkend and, crossing the Coleford road where the Parkend toll gate was later set up, went to Oakwood to serve Mushet's two Oakwood Mill iron ore mines. In about 1855 James and Greenham extended the tramroad further west to their China Engine and New China Level iron mines to enable them to bring the ore to their Parkend ironworks.

The Birches branch was built about 1812. It left the main tramroad about a quarter of a mile south of Parkend and went north-eastwards serving As You Like It and Birches Engine pits, the Independent pits and others on its way. After passing the *Rising Sun Inn* it joined the Moseley Green tramroad.

At the beginning of the tramroad era the machines for weighing the contents of the trams were at Lydney and Lydbrook, at the end of the journeys. Traders were soon complaining that the machines were inaccurate and cheating them, so in 1811 the Severn and Wye Company adjusted their machine at Lydney to weigh 120 pounds to the hundredweight (one hundredweight = 112 pounds). The Company soon discovered that traders were carrying more weight in their trams than regulations allowed and were damaging the track. As there was little point in discovering this at the end of the journey, in 1838 a weighing machine and keeper's house were erected at Parkend so that the overloading could be prevented at the start of the journey. The weighing machine was situated a short distance south of where the railway station was later to be built, between the road and the railway line.

In spite of criticism from traders, other railway companies and the Crown, the Severn and Wye Company delayed introducing steam locomotives as long as they could. The cost of converting the many miles of steep and difficult track would be great, and would reduce the comfortable dividends that the high charges they were making enabled them to pay. Edward Protheroe tried to persuade them to introduce a steam railway from Lydney to Foxes Bridge in 1840 without success. Mr. Nicholson, his lessee of the Parkend colliery, supported him in 1848 before a Select Committee of the House of Commons, which had been appointed to look into the management of Crown Woods. He argued that the existing tramways in Dean were inadequate, and strongly urged that branch lines of railway should be constructed, connecting the different works in the Forest with the main railway lines outside it. This, he said, would benefit the coalmasters, the consumers, and the Crown.

Railways

It was not until 1864 that the Severn and Wye Company introduced small steam locomotives on the main line tramroad. They were not satisfactory, so in 1868 a broad-gauge line was constructed by the side of the tramroad along the 8 miles from Lydney up to Wimberry Slade and was opened to traffic the following year. The double tramroad to Parkend and the single line beyond were retained. North of where Parkend station was to be, the new railway ran under the new ironworks covered way that had just been built, and then northwards with the tramroad on its left. The Severn and Wye Company bought land here, possibly cutting into the hillside, to accommodate the new track. This could not have been welcomed by Mr. David Rees who worked for the Parkend ironworks as an engine driver, and who in 1865 had bought land in front of the coke yard and built a cottage on it. Now a few feet in front of it, steam trains would run. Mr. Rees may have been reconciled to the noise from the coke yard behind him, and the covered way on his left, but the noise of the locomotives in front must have been a most unwelcome addition. Among the first goods carried on the new track was coal for the Parkend furnaces from South Wales via the South Wales Railway, to which the line was now connected.

On the stretch between Parkend and Cannop an accident occurred in 1869. A team of horses belonging to the Forest of Dean Chemical Company was pulling empty wagons on the tramroad down the valley from Cannop to Parkend. There was no haulier in attendance, and the leading horse crossed over from the tramroad to the broad-gauge railway and was killed by a train on its way up the valley. Later, after a similar accident the following year, a fence was put up between the tramroad and the railway.

Even though the Severn and Wye company had started to introduce broad-gauge tracks (7ft $0^{1}/_{4}$ in.), they were soon persuaded that standard gauge tracks (4ft $8^{1}/_{2}$ ins.) were the thing of the future. In 1869 they began to replace their broad-gauge tracks with those of standard gauge and ran standard gauge tracks over the remainder of their main tramroads. The conversion was completed by 1874.

The Marsh Sidings

At Parkend an elevated wharf was constructed near the beginning of the Milkwall tramroad branch, and four sidings were run from that tramroad to the top of the wharf so that merchandise could be tipped down into railway trucks waiting in a siding. The wharf was known variously as Parkend Wharf, Parkend Marsh, Marsh Wharf and Parkend Goods. South of the wharf, between the railway sidings and the road, was the goods shed.

A Severn & Wye passenger train at Parkend bound for Lydney in about 1922.

VIEW FROM CINDER TIPS, PARK END.

A view of the area round the station from the top of the ironworks cinder tips, which were removed by about 1908. Above the signal box, left, can be seen the *British Lion* pub, immediately next to a row of three-storey cottages. On the right, with a greenhouse in front, is the now demolished Parkend House, once the home of Thomas Hedges Deakin, first manager and then co-owner of Parkend Colliery. At the top right, the Castlemain Pit of that colliery can just be made out.

The Coleford Branch

At the beginning of 1875 a branch railway line to Coleford was laid from just north of Parkend. The junction was called Coleford Junction. It opened for mineral traffic on 19 July. It was a single line track, and, after winding past the sites of the 17th century King's ironworks and the stampers' works, followed roughly the Milkwall tramroad for the first part of its three-and-three-quarter mile journey to Coleford, climbing most of the way at a gradient of 1 in 30. The line crossed the Coleford road by an iron bridge (now removed) at Darkhill and, after passing the sites of both the Mushets' ironworks, went on to Coleford.

In the same year, 1875, passenger services were introduced on the line from Lydney. At noon on 23 September the Severn and Wye's first public passenger train left Lydney Junction for Parkend and then for Lydbrook. It carried the chairman and directors of the company. A cannon was fired to mark the event. It poured with rain during the whole of the journey. By the following month there were five trains a day in each direction from Lydney to Parkend, but by December the number was reduced to three.

On 9 December of that year the branch to Coleford was formally opened for passenger traffic. The people of Coleford had waited a long time for a railway to run to their town, and celebrated the day in a royal manner. There was a general holiday, the market place and streets were decorated with fir trees and evergreen arches, and at one o'clock a cheering crowd greeted the arrival of the train, its engine decked with flowers and holly. In the evening the streets were crowded with visitors from the surrounding villages enjoying the festivities and illuminations, and there was a specially arranged public ball.

The regular service began the following day. In January 1876 there were two through passenger trains each way between Lydney and Coleford via Parkend, as well as connections at Coleford Junction, but by 1879 there was only one through train each way, plus connections.

Parkend station had two platforms. It was to become quite a busy station, because eleven men were employed there in 1904. The passenger platform at Coleford Junction was between the rail junction and the road bridge which was removed in 1981. In 1889-90 it was provided with a shelter for the workmen in David and Sant's stone works (which were adjacent), who took tickets at the signal box. The platform quickly decayed, and was replaced in 1895. It was little used, and was closed in January 1906. The junction, however, was still used by passengers on certain trains going to and from Coleford, but no mention was made in the public timetables, and Parkend was the official place to change for Coleford.

Another branch line and two sidings must be mentioned. The Furnace branch ran from Coleford Junction across the Blakeney road parallel to the main line for a short distance and then on to the coke-yard on the hill to the east of the ironworks. In about 1887 it was extended to the Parkend Royal pits, and from then onwards the branch was also known as the Parkend Royal branch. A siding was laid to the Brookhall Ditches pits in 1873. Coal from them went to the Parkend ironworks. Finally a short siding was run from Coleford Junction to the Parkend Stone Works.

In 1879 the first Severn Bridge from Purton to Sharpness was opened, and in that year the Severn and Wye Company amalgamated with the Severn Bridge Railway Company. This Company – including what was left of its tramroads as well as its railways – was taken over by the Great Western Railway and the Midland Railway jointly in 1894 and, by the time the lines closed, they formed part of the Western Region of British Rail.

It is sad to reflect that by the time the railways arrived, the industrial health of Parkend was about to decline. Both the tinplate works and the ironworks, big employers of labour, were to reduce their activities in the next decade or so, and then to cease production altogether. As they, and the stampers, and the mines, and the quarries closed down, so the tramroads and railways were first left unused and then had their rails ripped up. The Birches Branch tramroad had been disused since about 1849, before the railway arrived, and was officially abandoned in 1874. The Brookhall Ditches tramroad was abandoned in the same year, when the railway siding was operative. The Milkwall tramroad lasted until 1876. The Ivy Moor Head tramroad to Parkend Royal pit still existed in 1878, although the sidings to Catch Can, Standfast, Staple and Parkend Main pits had gone. The Oakwood tramroad lasted until about 1914, but the track beyond the Oakwood foundry had been removed by 1901. After 1914 goods were transported to Parkend along the route by cart and pack-mule for a time, a return to pre-tramroad days.

The last tramroad in Dean ran from Bixslade quarries down to the lower Cannop pond. The last load of stone, weighing $8^1/_2$ tons, was brought down in July 1944; but coal continued to come down until November 1946, when the line was finally closed after 134 years service. The plates have now gone, but for long stretches the stones to which they were so long attached can still be seen. This is still an interesting valley and well worth a visit. There are derelict quarries at the top and on the way up a working quarry, several abandoned coal mines, a working free miner's level and a striking memorial to the men who died in the disaster at the Union Pit in 1902.

By 1901 only one of the four tips at the Marsh Wharf remained. There was enough traffic for this one tip for another six or seven years, but then it too closed. The wharf, however, continued to be used until the 1970s, and at times trade was comparatively brisk, with coal and ballast being brought in by lorry. The wharf was removed by the Forestry Commission in 1986 on the ground that it was unsafe.

As far as the railway was concerned, traffic ceased on the Parkend Royal branch in 1928, although the track south of the Blakeney road was not lifted until 1940; and the line from Coleford Junction to the Parkend Stone Works was removed in 1911. Passenger services ceased in 1929. The Foresters had never used them much and by 1929 a developing network of cross-country bus services had caused the railways to become increasingly neglected.

So ended the passenger lines of what the Foresters had called 'the Sad and Weary Railway'. However, freight was to be carried for nearly another 50 years, although after 1929 most of the double track became single. From 1949 successive sections of the line were closed. The line north of Coleford Junction was closed in August 1960 when Cannop Colliery ceased to produce coal. The branch from Coleford Junction to Coleford closed in 1967. From then on the Parkend to Lydney line was all that was left of the old Severn and Wye railway. Finally, in May 1976, that section closed too. The lines, however, were not taken up.

The Dean Forest Railway Society, founded in 1970, now leases Parkend station and the line southwards from the Crown. For a time they had their headquarters and rolling stock at the station but in January 1978 they moved down the line to Norchard, near Lydney, to the site of an old coal mine. From here they run a passenger line between Lydney Junction and Parkend.

Looking north towards the railway station with a temporary siding going off through a gate on the left into the ironworks cinder tips. These have now been virtually levelled, some 10,000 tons having been taken away largely in connection with building the New Road from Lydney to Lydbrook which can be seen beyond the gates.

A view through the station, a scene which has largely been recreated by the Dean Forest Railway. Of the original buildings only the goods shed remains but a convincing recreation of the station building has been erected.

Taken from the crossroads looking over the level crossing up one of the original routeways through the village the finger post pointing to Yorkley and Severn Bridge. Running right to left parallel to the railway is the New Road from Lydney to Lydbrook built in the early years of the twentieth century to open up the Forest to tourists. Whilst initially they travelled by horse and carriage and would have had little effect on the railway but once motorised omnibuses appeared after the First World War the railway began to lose passenger traffic.

The Cross, Parkend

Above. Looking north to the Cross in the 1930s. Parkend Signal Box can be seen on the right. The railway running across the foreground leads to the Marsh Sidings.

Right. The Marsh Sidings and wharf in 1982. In the ivy-covered house on the right Robert Deakin, Suffragen Bishop of Tewkesbury, was born and brought up.

Below Left. Looking across the Marsh Sidings in the 1930s towards the village and Castlemain Pit. Felled timber is being loaded onto wagons. The stack of logs marks the site of the original goods shed, moved from here to its present site at the station in 1897.

Below Right. Wagons being loaded with coal and pit props at the Marsh Sidings in 1962. The route of the connecting line to the station and its gentle gradient are clearly shown here.

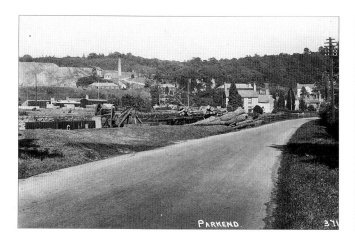

PARKEND.

– 63 –

An excursion train leaving Parkend in the 1960s. Despite losing its regular passenger service in 1929, Parkend station saw frequent excursion trains organised for school and church outings, trips to football matches and the seaside.

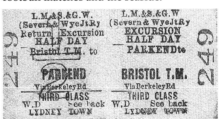

A 1930s excursion ticket for a half day outing to Bristol.

A ticket for an early 1960s trip to Barry Island. Again for a half day only it would have allowed for some time at the pleasure fair.

Left & above. A leaflet and a carriage window reservation sticker for outings to Porthcawl. Even in 1961 the fare of 13/6 (67½p) return from Parkend would have been a luxury.

It was traffic in ballast from quarries at Whitecliff near Coleford which kept the railway through Parkend open. Up until August 1967 this was taken by rail from the quarry and down the steeply graded Coleford Branch of the Severn & Wye to Coleford Junction. A reversal there brought the trains through Travellers Rest Crossing towards Parkend. A Type 1 diesel hydraulic 0-6-0 is seen above passing Travellers Rest Crossing Signal Box on one of these workings. With the closure of the Coleford Branch ballast from Whitecliff was brought by road to Parkend and tipped into the railway ballast hoppers at the Marsh Sidings. This was a daily working until Friday 26 March 1976 and the last trainload behind Sulzer Type 2 number 21 155 is seen below about to cross the New Road.

PARKEND... THE COLLIERY & SCHOOLS.   W.P.398.

Parkend Royal Colliery in about 1912. Parkend school appears in the right background.

Chapter 8
Coal - the Last Giant of Parkend's Industries

Iron smelting was the leading industry in the Forest's economy for over 2,000 years. Coal reached the same position at the end of the 18th century, but its paramountcy lasted less than 200 years.

The first record of coal working in Dean appears in some Gloucester records of 1282, but it is known that coal was mined there in small quantities in Roman times for use in domestic fires; some was found on the site of the Chesters Villa in Woolaston in the 1930s. The Normans also used it for their fires, but wood was still the main domestic fuel and was to remain so for hundreds of years. The Normans may also have used coal for roasting iron ore before smelting it with charcoal, a practice certainly followed from the mid-17th century until the invention of the coke blast furnace in the 18th century.

In the early days much of the coal that was mined in Dean was a by-product of iron ore mining, since the seams were in some areas found close together. It was also taken from the earth's surface where the veins of the mineral showed through (as in the case of iron ore), or from 'levels', which were passages made in the side of a hill. The passages ascended slightly, if this were possible, as this kept the level drained of water and facilitated the removal of the coal. Shallow pits, known as bell pits, were also sunk. Such pits would be abandoned as soon as they collapsed, and the presence of such collapsed pits accounts for the uneven state of the ground on the hill just east of Parkend.

In the 1550s the Forest was producing about 3,000 tons of coal a year, a seventieth of the output of the whole country. By the 1680s the figure had risen to 25,000 tons. Indeed, in the 17th century coal mining began to rival iron making as Dean's foremost industry, and businessmen from outside the Forest began to show an interest in Dean's coal. The Crown tried to accommodate them by attempting to curtail the rights of free miners and grant mining concessions to wealthy petitioners. In 1637 Edward Terringham was granted 'all the mines of coal' in the Forest for 31 years for a rent of £30. The free miners opposed this and other such leases and, while they did not succeed in preventing foreigners from mining in Dean, they at least succeeded in retaining their right to mine the coal themselves. As the 18th century progressed the demand for Dean coal increased. Forest coal mines were soon supplying coal to most of Hereford, to Monmouth and part of Monmouthshire, down the Severn to Chepstow and across it to Berkeley.

Throughout the 18th century new pits were opening. The first record of a pit at Parkend relates to one called Hopewell, which was opened in 1718, but it is not known where it was. Others opened in the Parkend area in the 18th century were Standfast, opened in 1722, Staple in 1726 and Church Hill, which was probably about three-quarters-of-a-mile east of Parkend, in 1745. Arthur's Folly was opened in 1774, and Catch Can (or Ketch Can, or Catch as Catch Can) was operating by at least 1783. By 1787 there were 121 coal pits in the Forest involving 662 free miners, but 31 of them were not working. In that year about 90,000 tons of coal were produced. In the same year in Parkend Walk (a larger area than Parkend itself – see page 17) 26 individuals and three groups owned 37 pits. It was suggested in 1788 that many of the pits in and around Parkend should be closed and the land enclosed and timber grown on it. Fortunately for the people of Parkend this suggestion came to nothing.

The big demand for Dean coal began at the end of the 18th century with the introduction of the coke blast furnace, which enabled coke to be used for iron smelting in place of charcoal. The extra demand required an improvement in the way coal was being transported: on the backs of horses and mules and in carts. The introduction of tramroads at the beginning of the 19th century made the transport of coal much easier. The pits became linked with ironworks in the Forest and with ports on the Severn and Wye rivers, and the coal industry in Dean was now able to expand and join the rest of England in the 19th century upsurge of industrialisation.

Up to now pits had seldom gone deeper than 25 yards, but in many parts of Dean all the coal near the surface had been mined, and it was becoming necessary to dig more deeply into the earth to reach the coal in the lower seams. Going more deeply often resulted in more water being collected at the pit bottom, and this made it necessary to pump the water out. Writing in 1779 Samuel Rudder, the historian, said that Dean pits 'are not deep, for when the miners find themselves much incommoded with water, they sink a new one rather than erect a fire engine', that is, a steam engine to pump out the water (steam engines had first been used for this purpose only a few years earlier). However, as the years passed, steam engines for pumping out water, as well as other modern equipment, became more necessary. But they cost money and the free miner could not usually find it. He was a small man – owner, organiser, hewer of coal and odd-job man, with no expectation of making a fortune, only wanting a reasonable living. So more ambitious, richer, men from outside the Forest stepped in and invested their capital in Dean coal. These foreigners could mine only if free miners leased or sold them their gales. Such transactions had occasionally taken place since the middle of the 17th century, but the practice became more frequent as the Dean coalfield attracted more foreigners. Doubts about the legality of such leases and transfers were removed by an Act of 1838.

Edward Protheroe

One such foreigner – perhaps the biggest – was Edward Protheroe. In about 1812 Protheroe, together with Thomas Waters, bought most of his uncle John Protheroe's collieries for 20,000 guineas. Among these were probably the Brookhall Ditches pits which were northeast of Parkend village. However, it is unlikely that he acquired all his Parkend pits from his uncle, because Nicholls says that 'by the spring of 1827 Mr. Protheroe effected the opening of collieries at Ivy Moor Head, Park End Main, Park End Royal Pits and Birch Well'. By Park End Royal Pits, Nicholls probably meant Parkend Royal pit (also known as Royal Deep and, later, as Castle Hill) and Land Royal pit. By 1827 Protheroe also owned Castlemain (sometimes known as Castlerag) and New Fancy, about a mile northeast of the village. Protheroe traded as the Park End Coal Company and he developed his pits as well as the

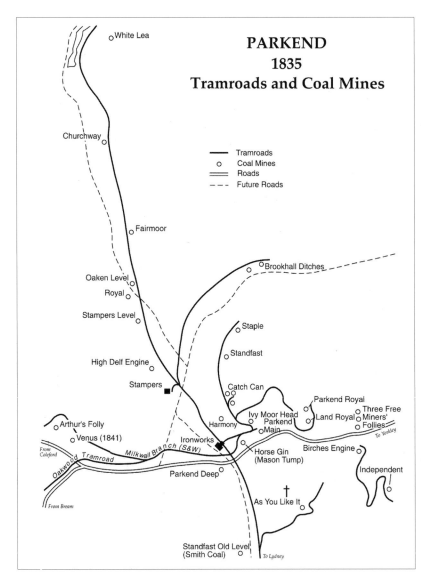

PARKEND
1835
Tramroads and Coal Mines

Tramroads
○ Coal Mines
Roads
Future Roads

mining techniques of the time allowed. In 1827 he erected a pumping engine and a winding engine at Ivy Moor Head. The pumping engine was probably an atmospheric engine, and was to survive until 1877 when it was reputed to be one of the oldest pumping engines in the Forest. He also erected pumping engines and winding engines at Parkend Main and Birches Well, and a winding engine at Parkend Royal; and in 1831 a pumping engine and a winding engine at the New Fancy. In 1827 he connected his Parkend pits to the main Severn & Wye tramroad by one of his own 1,500 yards long. In 1832 the depth of his main shafts at Parkend and Bilson varied from about 150 to 200 yards. In that year he employed 400 to 500 people in his collieries. By the 1820s coal from his Parkend pits was being sold as far away as Oxford, where, to this day, there is a Park End Street which commemorates the site of a wharf where Parkend coal was unloaded from barges.

However, Protheroe's interests in the Forest were not confined to coal mines. He acquired the Parkend Ironworks in 1824 and shortly afterwards began opening iron mines near Milkwall. In 1837 he built two blast furnaces at Soudley. By 1841 he held more gales in the Forest than anyone else, owning or leasing about ten iron mines and about ten collieries (not single pits) and holding shares in about twenty others. He also had interests in tramroads. He was, in 1809, one of the original subscribers to the Severn & Wye Railway & Canal Company, and later owned nearly half the shares. Soon he became its chairman and served as such until 1827. In 1826 he bought the Great Bilson Colliery and the whole of the Bullo Pill Railway, which by then had come almost to a standstill. He kept the

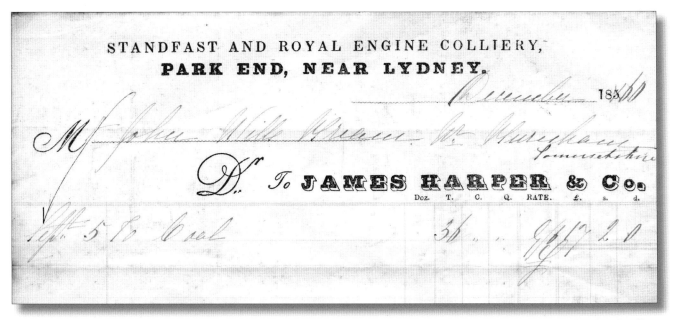

An early billhead for the Standfast and Royal Engine Colliery dating from 1860. The gales eventually passed to the Parkend & New Fancy Collieries Co. who held them as a pumping station to prevent water entering the Parkend Colliery workings. The gales had originally been in the hands of the Morrell family of Oxford.

Castlemain Pit with the screens on the left and with Parkend Royal in the left distance. At this date the two collieries formed one, Castlemain acting as the pumping station. On the extreme left the narrow gauge incline which brought tubs of coal from the Royal shafts down to the screens can just be discerned. The photograph was taken around 1900.

colliery, but sold the railway to a new company, the Forest of Dean Railway Company, of which he became chairman.

Protheroe was only one of the businessmen of the times who concentrated in his hands coal mines, iron mines, ironworks and tramroads, which were all interdependent. David Mushet and William Crawshay were others, but they impinge less on the story of Parkend than Protheroe.

In his diary for 1836 the Rev. F. E. Witts, the Rector of Upper Slaughter in the Cotswolds, tells us about a visit he made to one of Protheroe's Parkend pits. It was, he writes,

'one of the deepest and largest mines of the district, where the coal is raised from a pit nearly 200 yards below the surface... We watched the ascent and descent of the tram carts, as they were lowered to the bottom of the pit, or raised by steam with a heavy load of coal. From a workman near the pit's mouth, a finely bronzed fellow with intelligent and handsome features, a bright eye, curly hair and form indicative of great bodily strength, we learnt that the persons employed below including boys, amounted to 100, and that eight horses were used at the bottom of the mine who, once admitted, never saw daylight again till age or accident incapacitated them for work.'

The increased activity in sinking new coal and iron ore pits and extending old ones in the early 19th century took place with little order. There were no proper plans kept of the gales that had been granted over the centuries, so it was impossible to say precisely where they ran underground; and by 1830 disputes between coalworkers were becoming frequent. Such disputes in earlier days would have been settled by the Court of Mine Law, but that was abolished in 1777. Sometimes the disputes were about the boundaries of gales and related matters, such as responsibility for flooding, and sometimes they were sparked off by the fact that one party was a free miner and the other a foreigner - and foreigners were by this time becoming the principal pit owners in the Forest. The free miners' discontent was one of the factors behind the uprising in 1831 that had to be quelled by military force (see page 20).

So in 1831 the Government set up a Commission to investigate, among other matters, the mining situation in the Forest, including the allocation of gales, the causes of disputes and the complaints of free miners. Both free miners and foreigners gave evidence before it. Among the latter was Edward Protheroe. He told the Commission how he was developing his mines by introducing new equipment and went on:

'My works have an additional importance as being connected with extensive ironworks dependent on them for coal. These iron furnaces and forges have recently been erected at the cost of about £100,000 and the whole property is held under the rights and titles of foreigners. I may add, too, that upon both iron and coal works so held, very large sums belonging to ladies, minors and others have been advanced and secured by mortgage, and the whole value of the railways, in which £200,000 have been invested, would be sunk and lost by the destruction of the trade depending on our capital.'

Clearly big business (and hypocrisy) had moved into Dean.

Some of the most interesting of the documents produced in connection with the Commission's deliberations were large scale maps prepared by Thomas Sopwith, a mining engineer from Newcastle-upon-Tyne, which gave 'an exact surface and subterranean survey' of all the coal mines in the Forest. In the Parkend area Sopwith recorded the pits (except Venus) shown on the plan opposite. Venus Pit has been added, as this entrance to the Venus and Jupiter Colliery was opened in 1841 after Sopwith had completed his maps but before the 'awards' of that year were made. Hopewell and Church Hill pits, which were noted above as having opened at Parkend in 1718 and 1745 respectively, were not on Sopwith's maps.

The Parkend & New Fancy Collieries.

ADDRESS
&c.
T.H.DEAKIN,
MANAGER.
PARKEND

Parkend Aug 18 1885
Gloucestershire

The Commission took quantities of evidence and presented five reports to the Government. As a result of their Fourth Report, Parliament passed the Dean Forest Mines Act, 1838. This Act defined the rights of free miners and appointed a Mining Commission consisting of Thomas Sopwith, John Probyn and John Buddle to survey the coal and iron ore mining and quarrying areas of Dean and record the position of each gale.

The Parkend Collieries

In 1841 this second Commission reported. By their awards 104 collieries (as well as iron mines and quarries) were defined and assigned to free miners and other colliery owners. The written definitions, when seen in conjunction with the maps already drawn up, could leave no doubt about the boundaries of each gale. The awards defined nine collieries in the Parkend area. Those taking coal from the middle of the three groups of coal seams under the Forest, the Pennant Group, were the Royal, the High Delf Engine, and the Venus and Jupiter collieries. Above these, in the Supra-Pennant Group, were Oaken and Churchway, Standfast and Royal Engine, Catch Can, Independent Level, New Fancy and Parkend collieries. The Venus and Jupiter Colliery also mined at this level. Parkend Deep Colliery had a pit entrance in Parkend, but the mining area was situated a fair distance to the west.

The Royal Colliery was awarded by the Commissioners to James Brooks and Isaac Preest, a free miner. High Delf Engine Colliery was awarded to Moses Teague, a free miner. Venus and Jupiter Colliery was awarded to George and James Baldwin, who were also free miners (shortly afterwards the colliery was acquired by Sir Thomas Phillips and Edward Protheroe for £700). Oaken and Churchway Colliery was awarded to John Matthewman. Standfast and Royal Engine Colliery was awarded to James and Robert Morrell, who were bankers and the mortgagees of the colliery (the Rising Sun Engine Colliery, which included Arthur's Folly Pit, was also awarded to them). Catch Can Colliery was awarded to David Davies, Richard Hewlett and Edward Protheroe jointly. Independent Level and New Fancy were awarded to Edward Protheroe. Parkend Colliery, the largest in surface area and also in output of all those mentioned was also awarded to Protheroe. It included the following pits: White Lea with a branch called Ready Money, Stampers Level, Fair Moor Level, Ivymoor deep side of Catch Can, Birches Well Engine, Parkend Main, Cut out from Parkend Main, Parkend Royal, Brookhall Ditches and some free miners' Folly gales.

In addition to defining the area of each colliery, regulations were made to control the working of the mines and prevent further disputes and any repetition of the confusion that had previously existed. As a result of the Mining Commission's activities the mines in Dean could now progress and expand in a more orderly fashion than before.

After the coal awards of 1841 Protheroe's Parkend pits prospered. The three main ones now went down 100, 160 and 180 yards. In 1841 it was said that they were raising 90,000 tons of coal a year, although this figure seems high in the light of subsequent output figures for the colliery. The figure of 90,000 tons was nearly 20 per cent of the total output of all Dean's pits, which was 469,000 tons a year. In 1856, whilst the Parkend pits formed the biggest colliery in the Forest of Dean, their yield dropped to 87,000 tons. In the same year the 221 coal-works in the Forest yielded upwards of 460,000 tons.

By 1849 Protheroe had leased one third of the Parkend and New Fancy collieries to John Trotter of Newnham and one third to the Baptist Minister, Thomas Nicholson, of Yorkley. In 1849 he leased the remaining third to Thomas and James W. Sully. The Sullys were partners in a company of ship owners, colliery agents and coal factors in Bridgwater, Somerset.

In 1852 the Sullys, Nicholson and Trotter issued a prospectus for the formation of the Park End Colliery Company to buy the Parkend and New Fancy collieries. Their combined area was stated to be 779 acres, and the quantity of coal remaining unworked was estimated at upwards of 13 million tons, with even more in an underlying stratum. There were, the prospectus said, 'three pits in operation, namely the Royal Deep and Land Pits [presumably the Parkend Royal and Land Royal pits] and the Brookhall Ditches Deep Pit, and there are also two other pits commenced, one of which has been sunk to the depth of 74 yards and the other 40 yards'. The prospectus stated that the pits could yield 100,000 tons a year with ease, and that nearly that quantity was actually being raised at the time. It was proposed that the capital of the company should be £100,000, but probably not more than £80,000 would be required at first; the remainder would form a reserve to provide for the opening of new pits if they were needed. Prospects for the new company were bright. The Gloucester and Dean Forest Railway's steam rail link between the Forest and Gloucester would shortly be opened and this would increase the demands for coal. 'Should the present price of coal be maintained, which there is no reason to doubt, the profits of the company would at the assumed small vend of 100,000 tons per annum, furnish a dividend of 25 per cent; and should the vend be increased, as it might easily be, by opening fresh pits, the profits would be proportionately augmented'.

The Sullys, Trotter and Nicholson, whether they formed the Park End Colliery Company or not, did not buy the Parkend and New Fancy collieries because in 1857 Edward Protheroe died still owning them. However, they acquired them on his death. The Sullys soon took over Nicholson and Trotter's interests. They already owned the Standfast and Royal Engine, Catch Can and Independent collieries, and now traded under the name of the Parkend Coal Co. Most of the pits in Parkend had now been brought under one ownership.

In September 1871 after much unrest there were spontaneous strikes in Parkend and elsewhere in Dean and the Forest's first miners' trade union was formed. In the next few years the union was successful in increasing pay, reducing hours and securing other improvements in the men's conditions. But in 1874 the Sullys attempted to impose a 25% cut in pay. The union succeeded in reducing it to 10% but by the autumn the Sullys were back for another 10%. The men came out on strike and remained out throughout the coldest winter in 25 years. Finally, hardship and hunger forced them to compromise on a 5% reduction with a further 5% later on, and they returned to work in February 1875.

The reduction in wages, the strike and the consequent ill-feeling between masters and men was followed in 1875 by a slump. The drop in coal sales that resulted from it added to the Sullys' financial problems, for they had not been doing well for some time. They had found it necessary to take out a mortgage of £5,000 in 1871 and another of £6,000 in 1875. Others for £13,000 and £16,000 were to be taken out in 1878.

By that year James Sully was the only one remaining from those who had constituted the firm in 1857. In December of 1878 a limited company, called the Parkend Coal Company Ltd., was formed to acquire the collieries from him. Prominent among the subscribers to the new company was James Sully himself. He sold his collieries to the company for £40,000 and received 967 of the 1,000 shares issued.

The old company had not been very profitable; nor was the new one. It started off heavily in debt and new money was needed to sink the pits to lower seams, as the coal in the seams currently being worked was becoming exhausted. The continuation of the slump did not help, and in March 1880 when the banks would not supply more money the company closed the pits and threw some 700 men and boys out of work. In April the company went into voluntary liquidation.

Right: **A memo relating to coal being supplied to the Watlington Brewery, Oxfordshire by the Parkend Deep Navigation Collieries Ltd in June 1900 using the colliery company's wagon number 301.**

Below: **A letterhead for the colliery company dating from the 1920s.**

The year 1881 was an extremely tough one for the inhabitants of Parkend. In that year Sully's pits were closed, the tinplate works shut down for ever with a loss of two hundred jobs, and the last prospect of setting the ironworks on their feet was dashed. Unemployment must have affected every household in the village and, since the State in those days provided no unemployment benefit or other state assistance, only the workhouse, the misery and poverty in that year can hardly be imagined.

In May 1881 five of Sully's collieries were put up for auction: the Standfast and Royal Engine, Independent Level, Catch Can, Parkend and New Fancy. The first three were said to be 'of minor importance, though desirable for the protection of the Parkend and New Fancy gales'. The total area of the five collieries was said to be 1,240 acres, of which 1,150 acres were the combined areas of Parkend and New Fancy. (In the 1852 prospectus for the formation of the Park End Colliery

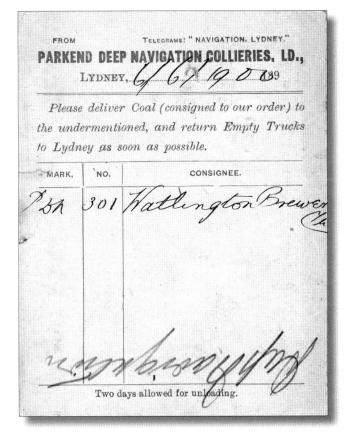

-71-

The base of the Castlemain stack with Parkend in the background, taken about 1925. The pumping engine house stands on the right, whilst the building beyond the stack houses an electricity generating set which provided power to the Parkend and New Fancy collieries. On the left is the Yorkley to Parkend road.

Company, the area of the two collieries was said to be 779 acres.) Among the advantages stressed in the notice of auction was the hardness of the coal and its excellence for household purposes. The output of the collieries in 1879, the last complete year before the pits closed, was said to be 101,198 tons. It was estimated that there were still eleven million tons of workable coal waiting to be mined.

The New Fancy Colliery consisted of one winding and one pumping pit. At the Parkend Colliery there was one pumping pit (Castlemain) which was 150 yards deep. Of the two Royal pits, the winding pit was 199 yards and the other 140 yards deep. The Birches Pit was 173 yards deep. Included in the package were other pits 'not at present in use'. These included Brookhall Ditches, Parkend Main and Ivy Moor Head. Ivy Moor Head was to reopen and was not to close until all the pits in the Parkend Colliery closed in 1929. No mention was made of the following pits which were part of Parkend Colliery in the 1841 awards: Stampers Level, Fairmoor Level and White Lea with a branch called Ready Money, although White Lea had been shown on a map of about 1874.

Included with the pits were the engine houses, the pit machinery (including engines, pumps and winding gear), and sidings, trams and horses. There was an enclosed yard at Parkend with stabling for 20 horses and a coach house loft, a fitter's, a smith's and a blacksmith's shop, a weigh house, and lodges, sheds, stores and offices. There were also 30 stone built workmen's cottages at Whitecroft, two at Standfast, two at Brookhall Ditches and one at Moseley Green (all with gardens), a bailiff's house with a large garden at New Fancy, and an excellent manager's house with stables, outbuildings, a garden and a paddock about one acre in area (probably Parkend House).

The passing of the five collieries to a new owner must have brought hope to the out-of-work colliers. As the Cinderford *Mercury* said in its edition of 17 June 1881: 'There are some rays of sunshine brightening the long commercial gloom of this district in the announcement that the Parkend colliery property has been at length sold and coal getting will be resumed shortly'. The new owner was a Mr. Jackson, reported to be from London.

Thomas Hedges Deakin

There now appears Thomas Hedges Deakin, who was to be long associated with Parkend and who is still remembered there. He was born in Pontypool in 1850, and began work in a colliery at the age of 13$^{1}/_{2}$ to learn practical mining. He was a teetotaller, a non-smoker and a Methodist lay-preacher. In 1877 he had become manager of Trafalgar, one of Dean's biggest collieries. Jackson now appointed him manager of his newly-acquired collieries in Parkend, and he took up residence at Parkend House. Under him the collieries began to work well; but in October 1883 they closed and over 600 men and boys became unemployed. The reason for the closure is not clear, but the collieries were heavily mortgaged. Later that year Jackson put the collieries up for public auction, and Deakin, together with Fanny Toomer and Susan Broadley bought them. But like the previous owners of the Parkend pits, the new partnership did not prosper. Fanny Toomer withdrew from it, and in April 1885 Deakin and Susan Broadley sold the collieries to a new company, the Parkend and New Fancy Collieries Co. Ltd. Its capital was £20,000 in 400 £50 shares, of which 125 were allocated to Deakin and 175 to Susan Broadley. Deakin became the company chairman, managing director and mining agent.

After the rough time they had had in recent years, the

two collieries now prospered. During the remainder of the 1880s they each contributed annually 80,000 tons of coal to the total Dean output of 720,000 tons.

In March 1892 the Parkend and New Fancy Collieries Co. Ltd. was wound up voluntarily and taken over by the Parkend Deep Navigation Collieries Co. Ltd., which had been incorporated in October 1890. Four thousand shares were allocated to Deakin, Broadley and the other former shareholders of the Parkend and New Fancy Collieries Co. Ltd. Deakin became managing director and chairman of the new company.

Deakin now entered the last phase of his career. It was to prove a prosperous one and he was soon to be the grand old man of Parkend. He received the accolade of respectability when he was appointed a JP and became the unofficial squire of the village. Men and boys were expected to doff their caps when they passed him in the village and women and girls to drop a curtsey. Woe betide any child who failed to show this mark of respect to him. Their father, if employed at one of his pits, would be told that it was in his own interests to ensure that his child showed due respect for the most important man in the village. He died in 1935 at the age of 85, working to the end, unwilling to relinquish his grip on his empire of collieries in Parkend and elsewhere in the Forest. He was buried in Parkend churchyard. He had been associated with Parkend for over 50 years. His work had been his life.

His son, Thomas Carlyle Deakin, succeeded him as managing director and continued in the post until 1942. Shortly after that he was ordained in the Church of England. Thomas Carlyle's son, Robert Deakin, was born in Parkend. At his death in 1985 he was the Suffragan Bishop of Tewkesbury.

Other Coal Works

After the coal awards of 1841 free miners continued to apply for gales, but in the Parkend area at least they were usually granted to mine coal in the deeper levels. In 1842 a gale was granted to Samuel, William and Isaac Preest called Skinner's Garden near the Brookhall Ditches; and in 1844 one was granted to Henry Beech and Charles Thomas called Church Hill, also near the Brookhall Ditches. The gale was surrendered before 1878. A Church Hill pit had been opened in 1745 but this was probably near Parkend Royal pit. In 1849 a gale was granted to Henry and William Phipps and John Morgan called Beaufort Engine, situated south of Parkend Church alongside the branch tramroad. In 1867 the Northumberland colliery near Skinner's Garden was granted to Edward Baldwin and George Burgham: and Durham Colliery, bounded by Beaufort Engine and Skinner's Garden collieries, was granted to James Billy. Some of these collieries were in the 20th century to become amalgamated into larger ones.

The difficulties encountered by Henry and William Phipps and John Morgan when they took out the Beaufort Engine gale are an interesting example of the conflict which could arise between an industrial concern and the Office of Woods representing the Crown. The men applied for permission to sink a pit on the gale and erect a steam engine, but the Office of Woods rejected their proposals on the grounds that they would be injurious to plantations and annoy Parkend Church and the parsonage. The men pointed out that the Venus and Jupiter Colliery was closer to plantations and the ironworks were nearer the parsonage than their gale; but despite offering to make concessions such as providing 'smoke consuming furnaces' the Office of Woods refused to yield. It was vital for the men to obtain permission to proceed as they wanted to because they had contracted to sell the gale to Thomas Stone of Bristol. In spite of their inability to persuade the Office of Woods, they nevertheless tried to get Stone to honour his agreement and buy the gale. When he refused they took him to Court and secured a judgement against him. Thus Stone became the owner of a tract of coal that was worthless. Stone managed later to dispose of the gale, but it was not worked until after 1907 when it passed to the Princess Royal Colliery Co. Ltd.

Amalgamation of Mines

As the 19th century progressed some pits became worked out and were abandoned but there was still coal in deeper seams. Some of it was difficult or impossible to get, partly because the gales were too small and partly because the galees were unable or unwilling to put up the money to exploit them fully. So the question of compulsorily amalgamating small gales into big ones arose. Once again it was a conflict between the free miners and the big financial concerns from outside the

Castlemain's pumping engine in about 1902. Installed in 1877, the engine drained Parkend Royal Colliery, Standfast Colliery and Castlemain Pit. It also took over the function of the atmospheric engine at Ivy Moor Head which was allegedly one of the oldest engines in the Forest.

Forest. The free miners saw no advantage to themselves in amalgamating their gales. Some, no doubt, would consider selling them for others to amalgamate if the financial reward were high enough, but others considered that their ancient rights to apply for and work small gales were being stolen from them by the activities of the foreigners. In fact, by this time it was arguable that there were few gales available that could be worked by free miners. Timothy Mountjoy, a miners' leader of the time, told a Select Committee in 1874 that every gale worth applying for had been taken up, and he 'would not give twopence halfpenny for those that were left'.

In spite of the arguments against amalgamation, the Government decided in 1884 to have legislation to amalgamate certain small gales (including Skinner's Garden, Beaufort Engine, High Delf Engine and part of the Royal) but the proposals put to Parliament foundered on the question of compensation for the free miners. Another attempt was made in 1903. On this occasion W. Forster Brown, the deputy Gaveller, said that the only difficulty in passing the legislation was 'in dealing with the free miners whose true interests also lie in the development of these gales, if only they can be made to realise it'. This time, the attempt to amalgamate was successful, and in 1904 an Act was passed, amended by a smaller one two years later, which gave the gaveller power to amalgamate 41 specified gales to form seven large ones. They were each of approximately 2,000 acres, sizeable enough to warrant the introduction of large amounts of capital to enable them to be worked on a big scale. These seven groups were subsequently worked by six companies, which included Parkend Deep Navigation Collieries Ltd. Another of the big six was the Princess Royal Collieries Company Ltd. which owned the following gales in the Parkend area: Southern United, Beaufort Engine, High Delf Engine, Venus and Jupiter 2, the Royal, and five others to the west, all of which were amalgamated in 1908 and called the Southern United Colliery.

Poverty and Strikes

As the 19th century advanced, more and more coal was dug and the coal owners became correspondingly more prosperous, but not a great deal of this prosperity seemed to come the way of the miners. For example, in the 1840s a miner's wage for a full week's work was 18 shillings (90p). Almost a third of this often went on rent. It is difficult to compare food prices in relation to the average working man's wage in the 1840s with today's, especially as spending patterns have changed, and the miner of the 1840s would no doubt grow his own vegetables, keep hens and perhaps kill the occasional pig. Even so an examination of food prices of the time suggests that they were on the whole higher in relation to average wages than they are today; and there is little doubt that after paying the rent, the collier had money only for the basic essentials of existence for himself and his family.

Employment, moreover, was not regular. Trade cycles produced booms and slumps, and disputes between employers and employees continually erupted. There were big strikes and lockouts in 1874-75 (already referred to) and in 1883, 1893, 1921 and 1926.

The 1926 lockout and the misery that accompanied it are still remembered. The mine owners in the country, including those in Dean, decided that because of falling exports it

A Parkend Deep Navigation Collieries Co. Ltd. railway wagon under repair at their wagon repair shed at New Fancy Colliery, probably prior to the First World War. The colliery company maintained a large fleet of wagons, around 400, to move their coal around the country and to the docks at Lydney, Sharpness and Newport.

was necessary to increase the hours and reduce the pay of the miners. When the miners refused to agree, the owners imposed a lockout from 1st May. The TUC declared a general strike in support of the miners three days later, but called it off after nine days. The miners considered that they had been betrayed by the TUC leadership. Nevertheless they were determined to continue the dispute alone. Dean miners received no money from their union as miners did in other parts of the country, because funds did not permit. Nor would the Poor Law authorities provide anything for them, only for their wives and children. Otherwise there was little else but what the local Miners' Distress Fund could provide from voluntary contributions, and soup kitchens, such as those Mrs. Deakin helped to organise in Parkend (what irony that Deakin caused the hunger of the miners and their families while his wife provided the soup to assuage that hunger!).

At first the miners were determined not to give in. 'Not a penny off the pay, not a minute on the day' remained their slogan; but their resolve gradually weakened and they began to drift back to work. The Dean men stayed out longer than those in any other coalfield in the country. At the beginning of December the Miners' Federation accepted defeat. The return to work was to be decided on a district basis and representatives of Dean miners and mine owners met at the Speech House. The mine owners showed no inclination to compromise and dictated their own terms. The miners had no alternative but to accept.

Many of the 6,500 Dean miners who had been locked out eight months earlier, however, did not go back to their pits. A fortnight after the dispute had ended, there were one hundred fewer miners at the New Fancy Colliery than before the stoppage, and this was typical of the general situation. The decline in the number of Dean miners continued: in 1929 there were 4,600 men employed below ground, in 1938, 4,100. Even so, when the mines were nationalised by the 1946 Act (the free miners' mines were excluded), half the Forest's male population still worked in coal. In 1947 the labour force was down to 3,800 and in 1955 down to 2,600. The tonnage of coal mined similarly dropped from 1,350,000 in 1938 to 521,000 in 1955. In 1965 it was 46,000.

Decline of the Coal Industry

The loss of markets and the consequent decline in the coal industry in Dean was mainly due to the cost of raising the coal to the surface compared with pits elsewhere in Britain. Most of the seams were nearly worked out, and the distance miners had to walk from pit bottom to working face added to production costs. Other factors were the large amounts of water that required pumping out and the variations in the thickness of coal within a seam. So the colliery owners found it difficult to sell their products in the market and the pits began to close, first one, then another. If there was ever hope that Dean could survive as a coal-producing area that hope was removed in 1959 when the National Coal Board issued its document *Revised Plan for Coal*, which gave its proposals for the future of Britain's coal mines. Dean was dealt with briefly: 'This small isolated coalfield has a restricted market and most of the readily accessible coal has been worked. It is unlikely that more than one colliery will be in existence by 1965 and even this is dependent on demand. In any event, the greater part of the existing labour force will be unable to continue in mining employment in the Forest'. And that was that.

The pits at Parkend, however, closed long before the National Coal Board came into existence. Parkend Colliery ceased to produce coal in 1929, but Parkend Royal remained connected underground with the New Fancy to provide that colliery with an emergency exit and Castlemain was kept open to pump water and provide air for it. The ruins of the engine house of the Castlemain shaft, which had been erected in about 1873,

can still be seen. The Castlemain chimney stack was blown up as an Army exercise in 1952. The villagers of Parkend watched the demolition, and witnessed the tragic death of young Leigh Goldsworthy who was hit by flying debris. The New Fancy Colliery ended its distinguished career in 1944, after having produced over $3^1/_2$ million tons of coal.

The end of the story of the Parkend pits came on 14 February 1947 with an advertisement placed in the Dean press by the deputy Gaveller. Addressed to free miners, it stated that certain gales were being surrendered by the Parkend Deep Navigation Company: the Parkend, New Fancy, Standfast and Royal Engine, Catch Can, and Independent Level – gales that had been household names in Parkend for almost a century and a half – together with a dozen other gales in Dean which had formed part of the Deakin empire.

The announcement stated in the time honoured manner that applications for the re-granting of the gales would be received at the deputy Gaveller's office, Coleford, at and after 10 o'clock on Monday 24th day of February, 1947. No-one applied.

The last of the large Dean collieries, Northern United, closed in 1965. All the pit shafts of the old Forest collieries have now been fenced off or filled in. There is practically no trace of their existence, or indication that below the surface are desolate, dark and empty tunnels honeycombing the ground, and full of foul water.

Though all the deep pits have long been closed there are still a few free miners digging in the Forest, much as their ancestors did. In addition, in recent years, there has been some open-cast mining by big concerns and more is possible.

New Fancy Colliery, about 1910.

Two views of New Fancy dating from the mid 1930s. By this date the majority of coal taken from the Parkend gale was being brought to the surface at New Fancy where it was screened and loaded onto rail. Today the site is grassed over and is the location of the Miners Memorial, erected in memory of those killed in the Forest's extractive industries, coal, iron and stone, and also a large scale explanatory geological map.

Chapter 9
Parkend Today

So came the end of an era in Parkend, one that began with such assurance and promise. It went out with a whimper, leaving Parkend with the debris of industrialism and no jobs for the miners. Some found fresh employment in the Forest, and some went further afield, as far as Gloucester. For others it was the dole. The Forest of Dean Development Association, which was founded in 1938, did much to introduce new industries into the Forest and expand and develop old ones. Some guest houses and bed and breakfast places have been opened to meet the demands of tourists, and a thriving garage has developed. Even so, the only organisations in Parkend today employing more than a few people are Forest of Dean Caravans and International Timber.

Forest of Dean Caravans began on the site of the Parkend Stone Works when the latter's lease expired. In addition to selling and transporting caravans, they also do general haulage. They have about 10 employees. International Timber, to whom reference has already been made in Chapter 6, employ about 24 people. The only other big organisation in the village is the Whitemead Leisure Park. This park brings visitors and trade to the village and is run by the Civil Service Motoring Association.

The coal mines, the ironworks, the stampers, the stone saw mills, the wood saw mills, have now all gone, but they leave traces of their former existence behind for those who trouble to look for them. Stand on Mount Pleasant and identify the places where the ironworks, and the tinplate works, once stood. Trace the routes of the railways and the tramroads. Find out where the leat joined the pond that supplied water to the ironworks. Go down to the lorry park, and find the site of the King's ironworks and where the stampers were active.

Walk round the village. Find the remains of the covered way and of Castlemain. Have a good look at the creeper-clad Dean Field Studies Centre building, which was once the engine house that supplied the blast for the furnaces at the ironworks, and which is now, perhaps, Parkend's most handsome building. How surprised would the architect be, who designed it well over a hundred years ago, to hear it so praised, concerned as he must have been at the time only with industrial efficiency. Look at the dignified proportions of the early 19th century building, whose stone inset proclaims it to be the *Fountain Inn*. Find out where the Square was.

Or take a walk in the Forest, and see if you can find where Nicholls's double oak stood. See what else you can discover: a mysterious rusty iron bolt, perhaps, found miles from any machinery; a small hole in the ground in the heart of the woodland, in which one drops a stone to discover it is an airhole for a disused pit; an isolated square stone on a footpath that shows that the path must once have been a tramroad. Where did the tramroad come from, where did it go to? What delight there can be in discovering these simple reminders of by-gone days.

Some debris from the past is an eyesore: the rusty wire that flaps dangerously from decaying wooden posts that border the old railway track but nature helps all it can. What must have been until recently hideous dark tumps of waste from the pits are now rounded and green and merge with the countryside.

Parkenders live in the present and for the future, but they are aware of their village's industrial past, and are proud of it. Parkend is a much quieter, less smoky place now than it was in its industrial heyday. In a world where noise and pollution are everywhere, is it not a unique discovery to find somewhere that has progressed from the sweat, grime and poverty that was Parkend, to a quiet backwater, where the only hazards are caused by sheep?

A late 1990s photograph of New Road, with the 1910 house on the left. Compare this with the 1930s view on page 52 Apart from the disappearance of the poplars on the right and trees in the background obscuring the church tower, little has changed. By 2009 a couple of new properties have been inserted in the area of the garage and and alongside the railway which runs behind the properties seen here.

This view looking across the centre of the village was taken from Mount Pleasant around 1905. Just below the rise can be seen the rear of the Square, with Fancy Road beyond. The branch line to Coleford, climbing away from Coleford Junction, is just behind the terrace of houses in the right background, then curving away in the centre of the picture to begin the even steeper ascent at 1 in 30 through Fetterhill and Milkwall. The sound of steam engines working hard up the grade echoed around the valley and could clearly be heard in the village. The Marsh Sidings are in the trees on the left and once there was a scheme to connect from the end of them onto the Coleford branch. Alongside the road curving away into the Forest once ran the Oakwood Branch tramroad which brought iron ore and coal down to the Marsh Sidings for transshipment.

The Memorial Hall and Fancy Road, looking towards Blakeney around 1930. The car is a gem – did it perhaps belong to photographer Gibbs? Travellers Rest crossing can just be made out in the right background.

Looking across The Square and the cricket field, to the shops and houses along the Fancy Road in the 1930s. The steam rising on the far left marks the site of Parkend sawmills. The Baptist Chapel can be seen in the left background, with *The New Inn*, now *The Woodman*, to the right. Behind this row, the Coleford branch line climbs up to the left, away from Coleford Junction. Modern central heating systems have done away with smoky household chimneys and better housing did away with all of the houses on The Square, in the foreground. Parkend is today a sylvan haven in the centre of the Forest, not the industrial community it still was in this view.

A famous occasion – Parkend beating Yorkley at cricket by 132 runs to 107 but when? Morton took the photograph, so it was sometime in the 1920s. Parkend had a cricket club from at least 1892.

Parkend cricket team, 1926, the winners of the Forest of Dean Cricket Trophy, photographed outside the Memorial Hall. From left to right : Back Row: Richard Thomas (Sec.), W. Richards, A. Hook, J. Ireland, B. Butson. Middle Row: B. Turley (Treasurer), T. H. Morgan, G. Gwynne, C. Morgan, R. Turley, G. Marshall, W. Turley, N. Cox, J. Bluett (Chairman). Front Row: G. Turley, W. Morgan, Alf. Cooper, Arn. Cooper (Capt), H. J. Morgan, G. Burrows, P. Edmunds. Boys – C. Hulbert, C. Morgan, N. Cooper.

Probably not many people realise today that the village fielded two football teams for many years, as these photographs show. The top picture shows the 1911-2 season Parkend FC eleven, whilst the lower portrait is of the Forestry School AFC team for season 1927-8, who were in Forest of Dean Division II and winners of the Coombe Tempest Cup.

MEMORIAL HALL   PARKEND.

The Memorial Hall was built in 1919 at the Bream end of Fancy Road, to commemorate those men from the village who had lost their lives during the First World War. The roll call of names of those who lost their lives can be seen just to the right of the front doors. This has now been moved to the left-hand wall with the Second World War casualties being listed in this location. Some of the funds for the erection of the hall came from the Parkend Institute, which transferred here from the Forestry School as that grew to occupy the whole of the old ironworks building. The Memorial Hall was erected on the site of an old warehouse and was the first of the memorial halls in the Forest of Dean to be completed.

The five First War dead were:
R. Burrows, died in France on the 27th September 1918.
H. Howells, died at Ypres, Belgium, 9th May 1915.
L. J. Hodges, died Rouen, France, 26th June 1918.
T. R. Moore, died 15th October 1918, Karlingen, Germany.
C. Mayo, died 11th October 1916, Doulleux, France.

Those lost during the Second World War were:
D. H. Bailey, 13th August 1945.
H. Griffiths, 12th July 1943.
F. G. Hardwick, 30th June 1944.
W. Jackson, 6th June 1942.
C. E. Preest, 12th May 1944.
C. W. Webb, 27th May 1940.

Appendix 1

Houses in Parkend in 1859

In the 1850s F. W. Dibben, an engineering surveyor, made a survey of all the properties in East and West Dean. The following is a list of the 76 houses he noted in Parkend in 1859. Where possible modern names of the houses that still exist are given to help identify them. Those with an asterisk have been demolished.

York Lodge
Whitemead Park Lodge*
A house at Oaken Level pit*
The *Railway Inn*
Deanfield
The Woodman
Seven houses in Hughes Terrace (the present 2 to 8)
Twenty-four houses known as the Square*
A house south of the Square (Brook House)*
Two cottages known as Furnace Cottages
Two single storey cottages adjacent to Furnace Cottages on the other side of the railway track* (site still identifiable)
The *Fountain Inn*
A house opposite the *Fountain Inn* (now the three Railway Cottages, possibly the oldest in Parkend)
Two houses (The Nook and Hazeldene) west of the *Fountain Inn*
Parkend House*
A house near the station, north of the Yorkley road and west of the railway crossing*
Twelve houses at Mount Pleasant in three groups of four (*only five remain)
The *British Lion* public house
The Vicarage
A lodge near the Vicarage* (foundations still visible)
A house next to the school
A house on Standfast hill* (foundations still visible)
A house near the Brookall Ditches pits (Woodside)
Turnpike house
Two houses at the Folly
The Folly Cottage
Four houses in Church Walk (Numbers 1 and 3, Rose Cottage and Woodland View. No. 3 was built about 1800)
A house at Birches Engine, 300 yards east of school*

In addition the house called Castlemain Mill, which in 1859 was one of the Parkend Colliery buildings, still stands.

The full Dibben's Survey with its key is at Appendix 2.

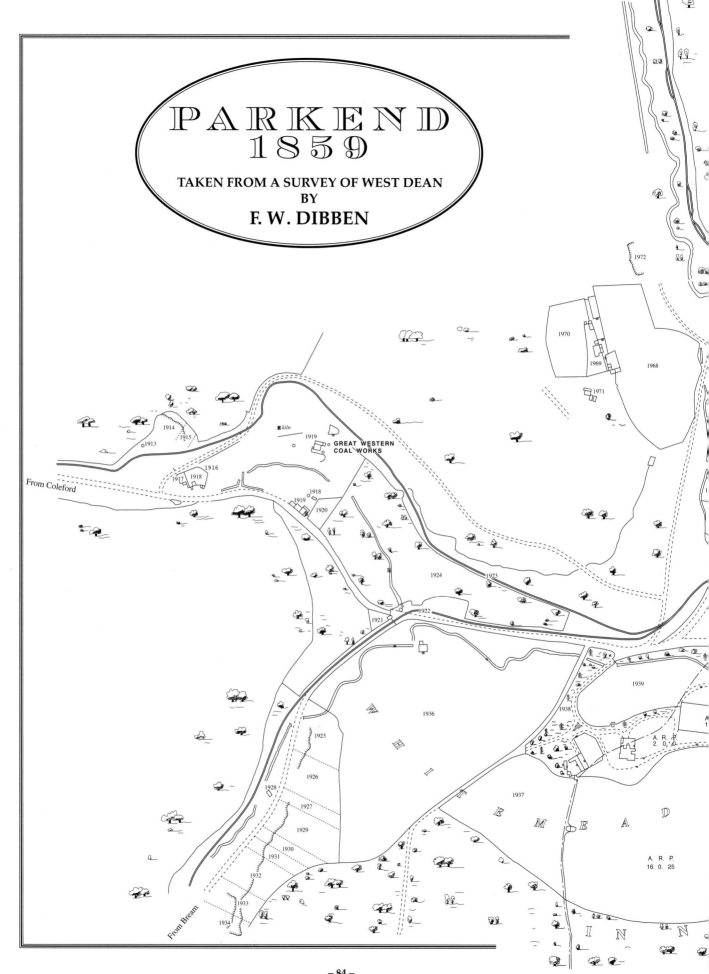

PARKEND
1859

TAKEN FROM A SURVEY OF WEST DEAN
BY
F. W. DIBBEN

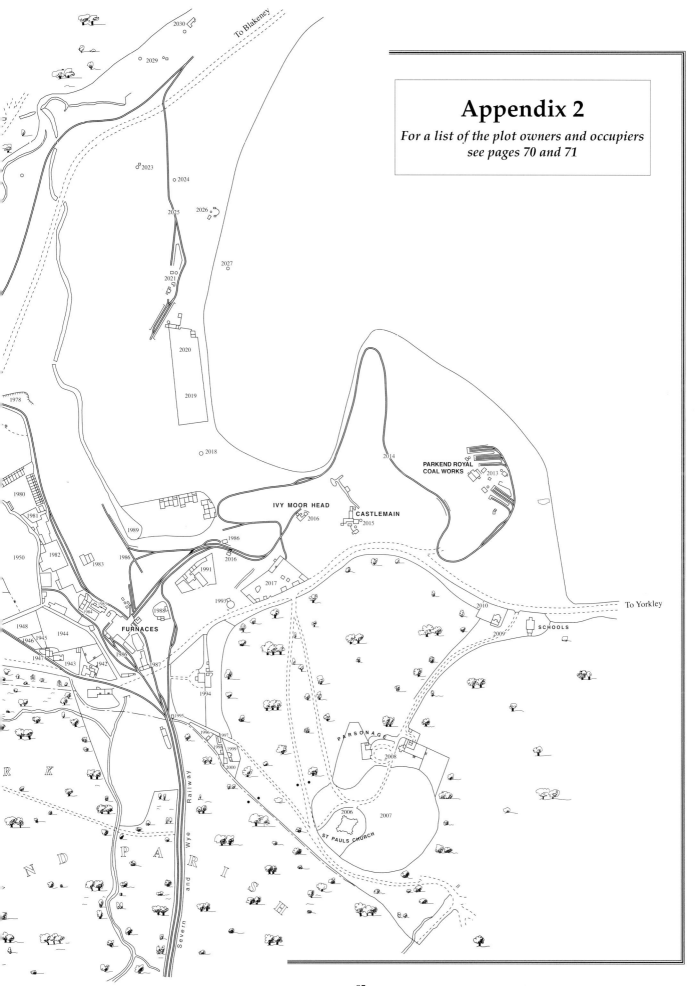

Appendix 2

For a list of the plot owners and occupiers
see pages 70 and 71

To Blakeney

2030
2029

2023
2024
2025
2026
2027
2021
2020
2019
2018

1978

1980
1981
1989
1986
1950
1982
1986
1983
1991
2017
1948
1946 1945 1944
1947 1943 1942
FURNACES
1986
1987
1994
1995
1996
1997
1998
1999
2000

1993
1988
1984
1985
1988

IVY MOOR HEAD
2016
CASTLEMAIN
2015

2014

PARKEND ROYAL
COAL WORKS
2013

2010
2009
SCHOOLS
To Yorkley

PARSONAGE
2008

2006 2007

ST PAULS CHURCH

Severn and Wye Railway

R K
N D
P A
R I
S H

Key to Dibben's Survey

Plot	Description	Owner	Occupier
1913	Pit		void
1914	Quarry		void
1915	Quarry		void
1916	Pit		void
1917	House & garden	Richard Morgan	Richard Morgan
1918	House, orchard & garden	Samuel Morgan	Samuel Morgan
1919	Great Western Coal Works	Great Western Coal Co.	void
1920	House & Garden	Great Western Coal Co.	Thomas Wright
1921	Turnpike House, garden	Comm. of D. Forest Roads	Joseph Hill
1922	Oakwood Tramway	Forest of Dean Iron Co.	Forest of Dean Iron Co.
1923	Tramway to Sling Pit	S&W Railway Co.	S&W Railway Co.
1924	Wood	The Crown	Sir James Campbell Bart.
1925	Quarry	Henry Courteen	Henry Courteen
1926	Quarry	John & Anne Morse	John & Anne Morse
1927	Quarry	Messrs. Trotter & Thomas	Messrs. Trotter & Thomas
1928	House	John Morse	George Jones
1929	Quarry	Joseph Williams	Joseph Williams
1930	Quarry	Thomas Priest	Thomas Priest
1931	Quarry	William Hoare	William Hoare
1932	Quarry	Walter Price	Walter Price
1933	Quarry	John Morse	John Morse
1934	Quarry	John Morse	John Morse
1935	Quarry	George Jenkins	void or George Jenkins
1936	Meadow, yard & shed	The Crown	Sir James Campbell Bart.
1937	Meadow	The Crown	Sir James Campbell Bart.
1938	Stables, yd, pt of gdn & shrubberies	The Crown	Sir James Campbell Bart.
1939	Meadow	The Crown	Sir James Campbell Bart.
1940	Plantation	The Crown	Sir James Campbell Bart.
1941	Fountain Inn, stables & garden	Edwin Kear	Edwin Kear
1942	House, orchard, yd, garden & meadow	Henry Kear	Philip Jones
1943	House & garden	Forest of Dean Iron Co.	Forest of Dean Iron Co.
1944	Field (arable)	Henry Kear	Philip Jones
1945	House, court & garden	Henry Kear	Roger Williams
1946	House, court & garden	Henry Kear	Owen George
1947	House	Henry Kear	Ellen Wintle
1948	Garden & sty	Henry Kear	Harriet Kear
1949	Blacksmith's shop	Harriet Kear	Richard Jones
1950	Meadow & garden	Harriet Kear	Harriet Kear
1951	Meadow	The Crown	John Nash
1952	Site for garden & house	John Lewis	John Lewis
1953	Garden	James Hughes	Rueben Ward & others
1954	Vacant grant	James Hughes	void
1955	House, orchard, yard & garden	James Hughes	George Rosser
1956	House & garden	Thomas & William Allaway	Thomas & William Allaway
1957	House & garden	]	
1958	House & garden	]	
1959	House & garden	]	
1960	House & garden	]} James Hughes	void, unfinished
1961	House & garden	]	
1962	House & garden	]	
1963	House & garden	]	

1964	Site of house & ground	James Morse	James Morse
1965	Stamping Mill & Tramway	James Morse	James Morse
1966	Meadow	Alfred Kear	Jno. Rogers & Messrs. Allaway
1967	House & garden	Alfred Kear	John Rogers
1968	Meadow	The Crown	John Nash
1969	House, orchard, yard & garden	The Crown	John Nash
1970	Meadow	The Crown	John Nash
1971	Carpenter's Shops etc.	The Crown	The Crown
1972	Quarry	Harriet Kear	Harriet Kear
1973	Quarry	John Nash	John Nash
1974	House	John Nash	Richard Heath
1975	Oaken Coal Level, office, tramway etc.	John Nash	John Nash
1976	Garden		
1977	Tramway to Brookhall Ditches	S&W Railway Co.	S&W Railway Co.
1978	Quarry		void
1979	Field	Harriet Kear	Harriet Kear
1980	24 Houses & yards	T & W Allaway	T & W Allaway
1981	House & garden	T & W Allaway	T & W Allaway
1982	Tinplate Works	T & W Allaway	T & W Allaway
1983	House & court	David Reece	David Reece
1984	House, court & garden	Forest of Dean Iron Co.	Forest of Dean Iron Co.
1985	2 Houses & courts	Forest of Dean Iron Co.	Forest of Dean Iron Co.
1986	Furnaces, yard, coke floor etc.	Forest of Dean Iron Co.	Forest of Dean Iron Co.
1987	House	Forest of Dean Iron Co.	Forest of Dean Iron Co.
1988	Garden, sties etc.	Forest of Dean Iron Co.	Forest of Dean Iron Co.
1989	Canal from Cannop Ponds	Forest of Dean Iron Co.	Forest of Dean Iron Co.
1990	12 Houses & gardens	Forest of Dean Iron Co.	Forest of Dean Iron Co.
1991	House, orchard, yard & garden	Edward Bowley	Henry Courteen
1992	Tramway	S&W Railway Co.	S&W Railway Co.
1993	Old Coal Works		void
1994	House, orchard, yard, gdn & meadow	Parkend Coal Co.	William Wintle
1995	House	S&W Railway Co.	William Train
1996	House & garden	Charles James Snr.	Richard Hopkins
1997	House & court	Charles James Snr.	Charles James Jnr.
1998	Orchard	Charles James Snr.	Charles James Jnr.
1999	House, orchard & garden	William Tippins	William Tippins
2000	House & garden	George Tippins	George Tippins
2001	Meadow	The Crown	William Lee
2002	Field (arable)	The Crown	William Lee
2003	House, orchard, yard & garden	The Crown	William Lee
2004	House, outhouse & garden	The Crown	Henry Gunter
2005	Meadow	The Crown	William Lee
2006	St. Pauls Church & Churchyard		
2007	Meadow	Rev. John Ebsworth	Rev. John Ebsworth
2008	Parsonage, offices, lawn & garden	Rev. John Ebsworth	Rev. John Ebsworth
2009	National School	Rev. John Ebsworth	Rev. John Ebsworth
2010	House & garden	The Incumbent in Trust	Edwin Lodge
2012	Birches Engine Coal Works	Parkend Coal Co.	void
2013	Parkend Royal	Parkend Coal Co.	Parkend Coal Co.
2014	Tramway	Parkend Coal Co.	Parkend Coal Co.
2015	Castlemain Pumping Engine	Parkend Coal Co.	Parkend Coal Co.
2016	Ivy Moor Head Pumping Eng & weigh.	Parkend Coal Co.	Parkend Coal Co.
2017	Workshops, stables & yard	Parkend Coal Co.	Parkend Coal Co.
2018	Pit	Parkend Coal Co.	Parkend Coal Co.

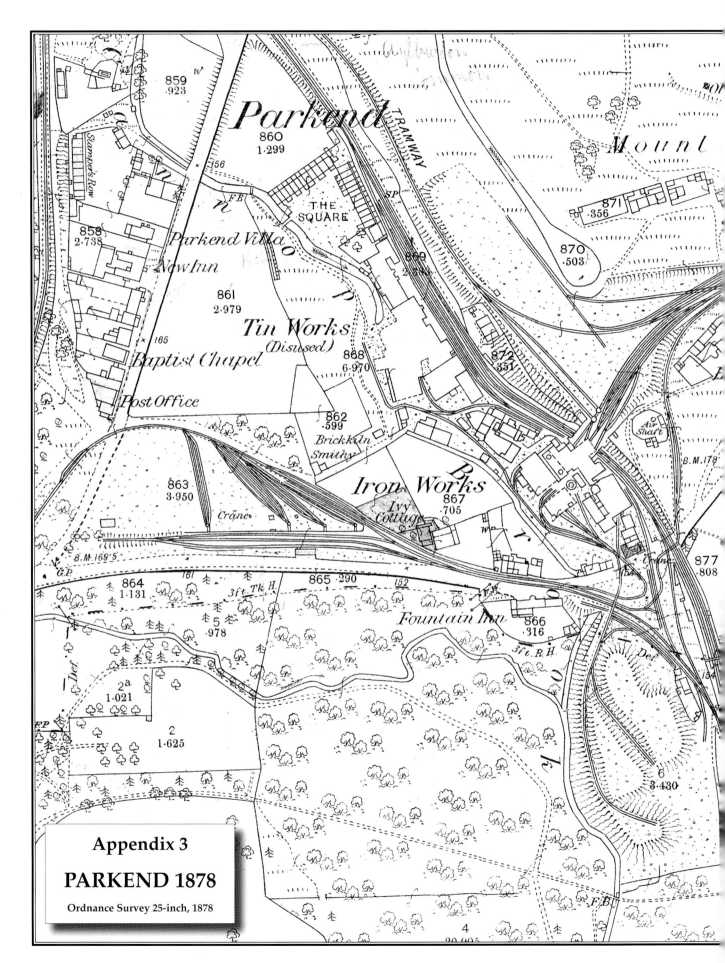

Appendix 3

PARKEND 1878

Ordnance Survey 25-inch, 1878

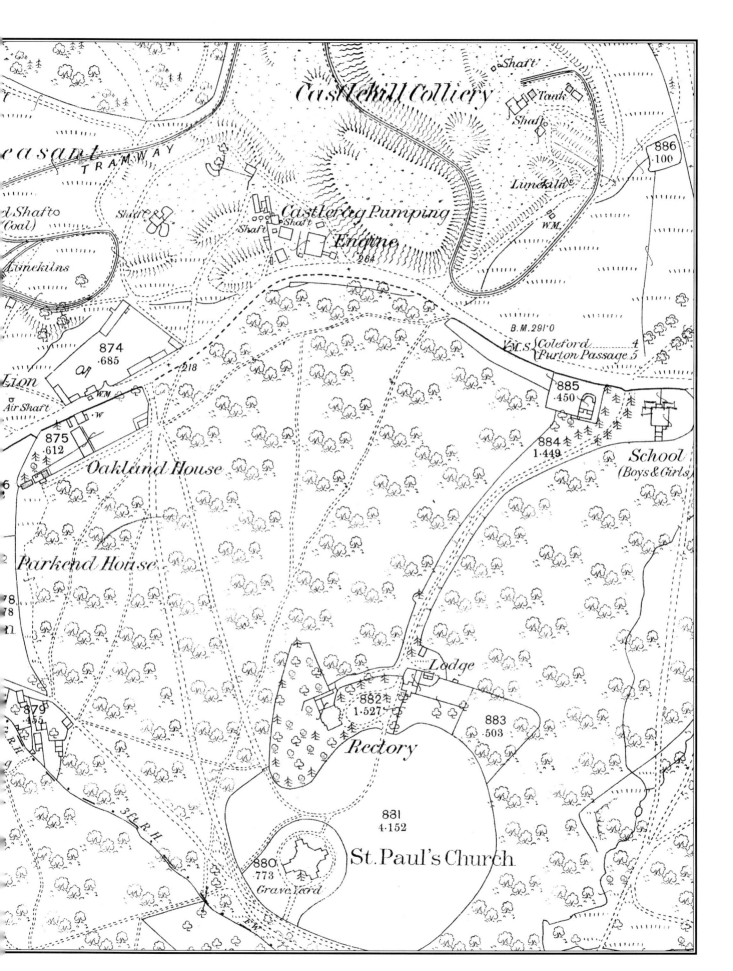

Castlehill Colliery

Shaft

Tank

Shaft

886
·100

TRAMWAY

easant

Lunekiln

d Shaft
(Coal)

Shaft

Castlerag Pumping

Shaft

Shaft

Engine

W.M.

·264

Limekilns

B.M. 291·0

V.M.S Coleford........4
        Purton Passage 5

874
·685

·218

885
·450

Lion

WM.

W

Air Shaft

884
1·449

School
(Boys & Girls)

875
·612

Oakland House

Parkend House

Lodge

882
1·527

883
·503

879
·155

Rectory

R.H.

3 ft R.H.

881
4·152

880
·773

St. Paul's Church

Graveyard

F.W.

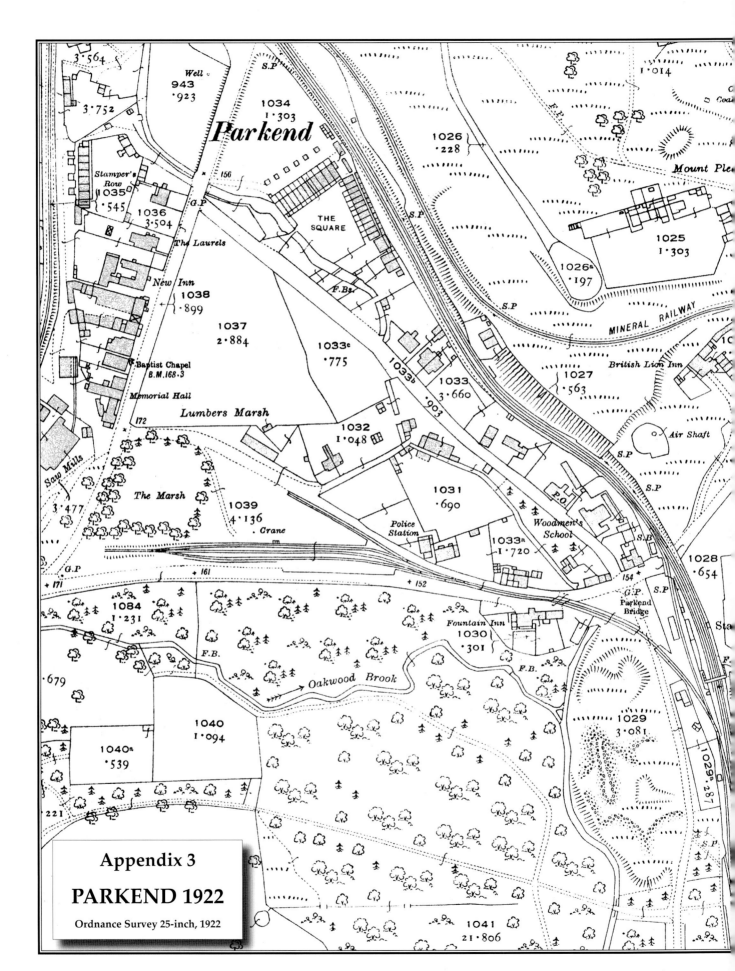

Parkend

Well
943
·923

3·564

3·752

1034
1·303

Stamper's
Row
1035
·545

1036
3·504

S.P

156

G.P

The Laurels

New Inn
1038
·899

THE
SQUARE

F.Bs

1037
2·884

Baptist Chapel
B.M.168·3

Memorial Hall

172

Lumbers Marsh

1033ᶜ
·775

1033ᵇ

1033
3·660
·903

1032
1·048

Saw Mills

3·477

The Marsh

1039
4·136

· Crane

1031
·690

Police
Station

1033ᵃ
1·720

P.O

Woodmen's
School

S.B

G.P

171

161

152

154

G.P
Parkend
Bridge

S.P

1084
1·231

F.B.

·679

Fountain Inn
1030
·301

F.B.

Oakwood Brook

1040
1·094

1040ᵃ
·539

1029
3·081

·221

1041
21·806

1026
·228

Mount Ple

1025
1·303

1026ᵃ
·197

S.P

S.P

MINERAL RAILWAY

British Lion Inn

1027
·563

Air Shaft

S.P

S.P

1028
·654

S.P

1029ᵃ
·287

S.P

1·014

Coal

10

Sta

F

Appendix 3

PARKEND 1922

Ordnance Survey 25-inch, 1922

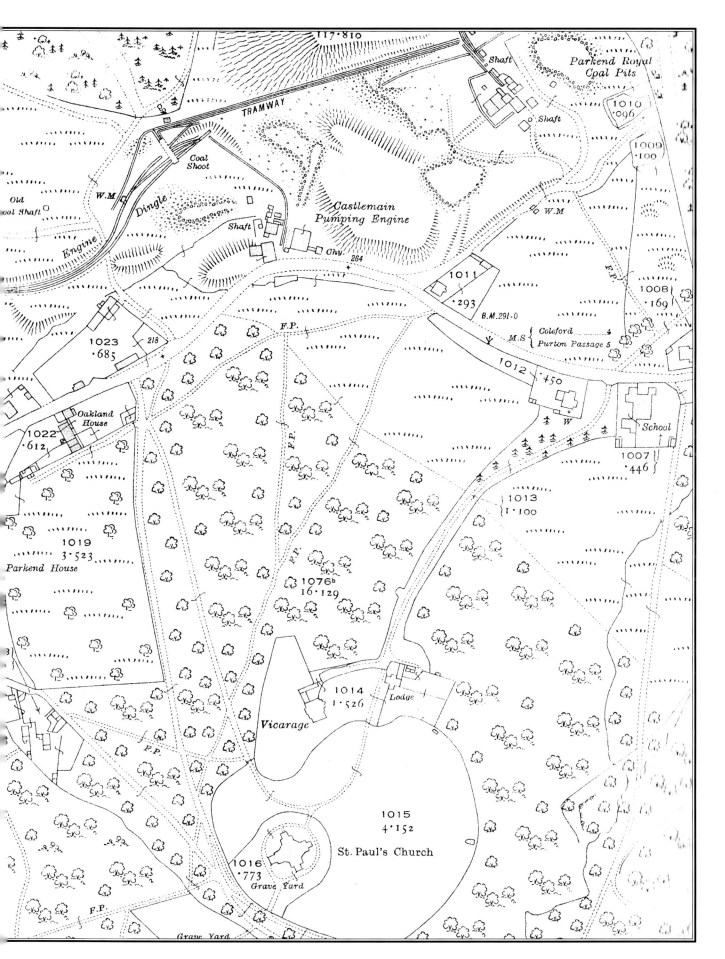

117·810

Parkend Royal Coal Pits

Shaft

1010
·096

1009
·100

TRAMWAY

Shaft

Coal
Shoot

W.M

Engine

Dingle

Shaft

Castlemain
Pumping Engine

W.M

Old
Coal Shaft

Chy

264

1011
·293

B.M.291·0

W.M

F.P

1008
·169

M.S

Coleford
Purton Passage 5

1012 ·450

F.P.

1023
·685

218

School

W

1007
·446

Oakland
House

1022
·612

1013
I·100

1019
3·523

Parkend House

1076ᵇ
16·129

1014
1·526

Lodge

Vicarage

1015
4·152

St. Paul's Church

1016
·773

Grave Yard

F.P.

Grave Yard

Books Consulted

The Industrial History of Dean	Cyril Hart
The Commoners of Dean	Cyril Hart
The Free Miners of the Forest of Dean	Cyril Hart
Royal Forest	Cyril Hart
Archaeology in Dean	Cyril Hart
Laws of Dean	Cyril Hart
The Forest of Dean	Rev. H. G. Nicholls
Iron Making in Olden Times	Rev. H. G. Nicholls
Personalities of the Forest of Dean	Rev. H. G. Nicholls
The Severn & Wye Railway	H. W. Paar
An Industrial Tour of the Wye Valley and the Forest of Dean	H. W. Paar
Parkend's Covered Way*	H. W. Paar
The Severn & Wye Railway Volume 1	I. Pope, P. Karau & R. How
The Old Industries of Dean	David Bick
Dean Forest Park Guide	HM S O
Dean Forest Railway Guide and Stock Book	M. J. Harding
The King's Ironworks in the Forest of Dean 1612-1674.**	H. R. Schubert
The Rise of the British Coal Industry	J. U. Nef
The Story of the Mushets	F. M. Osborn
Laws of the Dean Forest	J. G. Wood
Sixty-Two Years in the Life of a Forest Collier	Timothy Mountjoy
Geology of the Forest of Dean Coal and Iron Ore Field	F. M. Trotter
Custom, Work and Market Capitalism	Chris Fisher
The Diary of a Cotswold Parson	Rev. F. E. Witts
British Coalminers in the Nineteenth Century: A Social History	John Benson
Oxfordshire Local History Association Magazine, Vol. 3	
The Victoria History of the County of Gloucester, Vols II and V	

Also consulted: the archives of Forest of Dean Newspapers Ltd, and documents in the deputy Gaveller's office in Coleford, in the Gloucestershire Record Office and in the Public Record Office at Kew.

* The Forest Venturer: Journal of the Dean Forest Railway Society, No. 27, 1978.
**Journal of the Iron & Steel Institute Vol. 173, 1953.

Index

A view in Knockley Woods, Parkend, about 1910.

A short distance up the hill past the old Turnpike house on the Coleford road is a group of houses known as The Folly. They used to be shaded by this mighty oak tree but it became a danger to road traffic and in 1955 had to be felled. The last few moments of its life are recorded in this view.